Feeling Impact

Dedication

To my Father & Mother
Here's to more nights dancing among the stars.
Thank you

Feeling Impact:
A Timedancer's Study
of Irish Step Dance

Russell Patrick Brown Ph.D

Feeling Impact:
A Timedancer's Study of Irish Step Dance

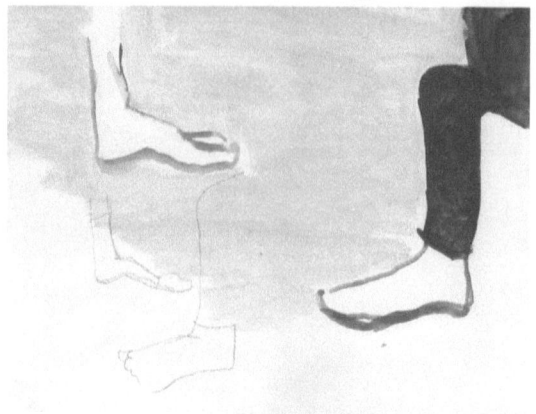

Feeling Impact: A Timedancer's Study of Irish Step Dance

A dissertation submitted to the Faculty of Arts, Humanities and Social Sciences in candidacy for the degree of Doctor of Philosophy, 2024.

Irish World Academy of Music & Dance,
University of Limerick, Limerick, Ireland.

Author: Russell Patrick Brown

Primary Supervisor: Dr Breandán de Gallaí
Secondary Supervisor: Dr Catherine E. Foley

Artwork: Jackie Askew. Design and layout: Michael D. Walsh

Copyright © 2025 by Russell Patrick Brown

All Rights Reserved

ISBN: 979-8-218-82520-1

Contents

Preface	1
Abstract	7
Acknowledgements	9
Chapter One: Introduction	15
Thesis Layout	17
Considerations	21
Chapter Two: An Draoí	29
The Trickster: Situating Self & Practice	31
Paraphrase	32
The Storyteller	34
The Druid: Entering an Arts Practice Tradition	41
To an Otherworld: Entering a Liminal Discipline	43
The Magician: Outlining Research Methodology	50
Defining Dance Research	55
A First Person, a Second and a Third: Building responsible reflexes in practice	58
The Augur: Theoretical Frameworks/Underpinnings	62
My Introduction to Performance Studies	62
Defining Performance, Practice and the Body	65
Summary	70
Chapter Three: The Psychometrist	73
Reverse Psychometry	77
Paraphrase	77
The Gay: Queer, Trans, Feminist Somatechnics	79
The Disabled: Stepping in Vogue at the Blue Teapot	90
The Traumatized: Trauma Exposure and Encounter	97
The Romungro: Kalipen and Romani Techno-Witchcraft	102
Summary	112

Chapter Four: The Querist 115
  Words on Caution 115
  Introduction 117
  Posing the Question 119
    Paraphrase 119
  Development 126
    UCD: Winter/Spring 2017 126
    On the Silencing of Shoes 133
    Asking in Motion 134
    Iveagh Fitness: 2016/2017 135
    MoKS: August 2017 139
    Production 143
  Aftermath 151
  Summary 154

Chapter Five: AngelAI 157
  On Kalipen in Irish Step Dance 160
    Paraphrase 161
    Dancing under Techno-lords 163
  Development 167
    The Village: 2019–2023 169
    Pumpkin Hollow: October 2023 174
    Clare: October-November 2023 178
  Production 184
  Aftermath 186
  Summary 190

Chapter Six: Cuir Síos (Conclusion) 193

  Reference List 200

List of Appendices

Appendix 1 – Performance Presentations,
see Google Drive Link:

https://drive.google.com/drive/
folders/115cF5RPTLd2lmRCH9rb9Vp7EDaLSndwr?usp=sharing

Copyright © 2024 by Russell Patrick Brown

All Rights Reserved

The Querist – Irish World Academy of Music and Dance, University of Limerick, Clare (September 20, 2017)

AngelAI – Irish World Academy of Music and Dance, University of Limerick, Clare (November 16, 2023)

Reviews of Feeling Impact ...

A compelling, original contribution to dance studies, this marvellous book explores *"impact-driven dance"* as a mode of intimate violence that requires contending with force as a vector for performance-making. Rendering dance as a site of exploration, creation, destruction, and general undoing, this book asks large questions of practice and memory, culture and trauma, including: "What are we willing to ask of history?"

The book lays out any manner of inquiry and research design, moving through personal reflection, medical treatments, psychotherapies, stories of family and kinship, and analytic descriptions of creative processes and outcomes realized in performance. The array of thinking across disciplinary formations offers the reader generous approaches to rendering dance practice as a relational field of force, mobilized through history.

Dr Thomas F. DeFrantz

Professor of Performance Studies & Theatre, Northwestern University; Director, SLIPPAGE: Performance | Culture | Technology.

This is a groundbreaking PhD thesis. It is revolutionary in terms of both research and how this is communicated. Using an Arts Practice methodology, Russell offers a profound exploration of Irish step dance through the somatic and felt experience and eloquently and poetically blends an academic insight in a way that resonates universally across communities of practice.

The thesis moves beyond traditional interpretations of percussive dance by introducing new ways of knowing – capturing not only the kinetic but also the intimate, sensory impact of dance history.

Through the performative outputs *The Querist* and *AngelAI*, the research touches on themes of violence, colonisation, and oppression, providing a deeply personal yet universally relevant lens for understanding the evolution of Irish step dance.

This work offers us a model for integrating personal narrative with scholarly inquiry, demonstrating how the body, identity, and history intersect in ways that can teach us all to rethink the boundaries of academic research. It is a compelling and compassionate invitation to embrace new ways of perceiving dance and history.

Dr Breandán de Gallaí

Course Director (BA Irish Dance; MA Irish Traditional Dance Performance), Irish World Academy, University of Limerick; Choreographer; Artistic Director, Ériu Dance Company.

When it comes to Irish dance, words like "dazzling" typically refer to the intricate footwork and heart-racing stamina of someone dancing their heart out on stage. Yet I can think of no better word to describe this discussion/book? by Queer, Romani, Disabled, Irish and Irish American Techno-witch step dancer Russell Patrick Brown.

With us on board, Brown "choreo-navigates" his way through waves of academic discourse, registering the violent impact of capitalist, white, patriarchal and colonial systems on Irish step dance and on his personal and ancestral histories -- as well as impact dance's capacities to redirect the "intimate violence" of self and surface that happens in "the moment of contact between foot and ground."

Brown is a riveting storyteller, and he tacks skillfully from topic to topic and place to place: from dancing on docks in New York to studios in Dublin and Limerick; from his Romani family and ancestry to his friends in County Clare; from loneliness as a form of traumatic stress to his family as a "culture of unbroken intergenerational somatic intimacy"; from the support he is given to Step&Vogue in the House of LaBeija to his understanding of "the process of studying something in motion as a form of *draíocht*" -- Irish for magic; from the challenges of his individual PTSD narrative storytelling treatment to collective, shared, intergenerational and cultural trauma in "our ever-evolving post/colonial world."

Throughout this potentially dizzying journey, Brown holds our focus on the impact of *feeling*. He forwards, alongside scathing critiques of academia, brilliant academic analyses of colonizing attempts at the erasure of ways of knowing through feeling, insistently registering the import of "expert intuition" in Romani and Irish ways of knowing and in the domains of the somatic at large.

Feisty, vulnerable, angry and full of love for his communities and for dance, Brown's *Feeling Impact: A Timedancer's Study of Irish Step Dance* is a delightfully provocative personal narrative intellectual tour-de-force of Arts Practice research that is, in a word, dazzling.

Dr Jacqueline Shea Murphy

Professor of Dance, University of California, Riverside; author of *Dancing Indigenous Worlds* (University of Minnesota Press, 2022).

Preface

I am asking you, in reading this book, to go against what many of us have been taught to believe about our bodies and what it means to study "us." Most of us have come to understand dance as a fleeting amusement—here to be enjoyed in one moment, gone the next. Many scholars liken dance to ephemera: print materials like political pamphlets, tickets, postcards, broadsides—the internet before the internet. Some of them argue this is dance's power: that it resists capture, that it escapes.

A decade since I began the journey of making this book, I agree that dance resists domination in ways other art forms cannot. But it is not fleeting. In my study of dances of impact, I have come to understand that dance is the most enduring act we perform. To study dance is to shake, stomp and jump at the very foundations of who we are—and we have been doing it for a very long time.

As we ask who we are and where we are going, within academia, the study of dance asks these questions in motion with all that it is to be human. As we explore how to live sustainably and with kindness and fairness upon our Earth, dance has always known the way. It gives us tools to investigate our most pressing challenges and our most pleasurable pursuits.

This knowledge came to me through a quiet, profound road I never intended to follow: recognizing my Romani identity and what that means for how I have lived and continue to live my life. The ongoing suppression, appropriation and erasure of Romani lives and Romani culture is an unforgiving, unescapable teacher. If you want to understand the colonization of dance and the subjugation of its power, heart and wisdom, study the colonization of Romani culture. In intellectual property law, arts funding and academic research, dance typically receives few legal protections, small resources and little respect. This would seem to suggest the limited value of dance as a whole.

I know from being Romani that knowledge that is misunderstood is, in a way, protected. It is not a good form of protection, but when there are no paths for liberation, few methods of self-preservation remain. For centuries, the study of our culture in academia has been a colonial endeavor called "Gypsy Lore" studies: an exotic field of study preserved mostly for white, English-speaking men. Othering, misinterpretation, racism, superstition and lust obscure fields of view for colonizers and have allowed many of our traditions and values to remain unexploited, even as we ourselves are exploited. This house of horrors has been a stern, stalking lecturer, mentor and witness to my research and to my life.

In my travels in North America and Northern Europe, I have found many people who share experiences of oppression, though their ways of resisting, surviving and thriving can differ in response to the many methods of dispossession and annihilation that continue to shape our lives. Our small conferences of hope, on the edges of academic symposia, theater lobbies, crowded cafés and protest marches, have been a refuge and a method of freedom for me. In gratitude from my little corner of the Romani world, I give back *impact-driven dance.*

For so many of us, violence is not distant—it is intimately applied by governments, businesses, and schools of hate to our lives and to our bodies. Irish Step Dance, Flamenco, Ballet Folklórico, African-American Tap Dance and other percussive dance forms have been and continue to meet this abiding terror. If this is new to you, I call you to explore it. If you have known this for as long as you have been dancing, I offer this book in solidarity. Your work—your dance—shakes our earth. We need it.

After observing blatant racism and colonialism in the most prestigious universities, the continued suppression of Romani voices, artists and dancers in the arts, and the continual exploitation of writers and researchers in academic publishing,

I decided to publish my doctoral dissertation (accepted without corrections) in full here. No words from the original dissertation have been removed or altered.

I was fortunate to land at the University of Limerick Irish World Academy of Music and Dance, Arts Practice PhD program, and this collective of academic revolutionaries gave me the enormous privilege of a wild, rigorous floor upon which to beat out my questions. Typically, once completed, PhDs of "high standards" are transformed for broader consumption. I felt this would be dishonest. My messy, fragile journey through the process of making a dancing PhD was, indeed, the work itself. Contortions around systemic hardship, leaps over appropriation, and rehearsals through betrayal are captured in these pages. The resulting score might be a path others can follow so that our centers of knowledge production do not close to everyone, but remain open and, hopefully, expand.

I did, however, add this introduction, the reviews and a public-facing title and subtitle. Doctoral dissertations are seldom read outside of academia, so their titles are typically written for a specialized audience. The academic title of this book, *Intimate Violence: Feeling Impact in Irish Step Dance*, was no exception. Yet "violence," in all its intimacies, is too easily misread in the wrong context. I prefer that, if the phrase intimate violence invokes anything for you, it happens within the care and rigor of the work itself—not by a passing glance at a spine on a kitchen table.

For that reason, *Feeling Impact*—the core practice-based output of this work—has moved from subtitle to title. As this text transforms from academic PhD dissertation to (hopefully) a guide for impact-driven dancers, in its place the subtitle now begins with a new identity: *the Timedancer*. When I argue that intimate violence echoes throughout all times, I do not refer to time-travelling cruelty, but to the power of those who are listening, watching and feeling across the ages. *The Timedancer* embodies impossible pasts in this moment so that all times may find new potential for community, care and creativity. It is for you that this text has been transformed—for all those feeling the call inside.

The Timedancer is also the name I now give to the work that continues beyond these pages. What began as a doctoral question—how impact becomes knowledge through the body—has grown into a living field of art, research and technology. Through *Timedancers*, I work to decolonize destiny: to remember that movement, not machinery, was humanity's first technology—the way we learned to transmit memory, measure time and make meaning together. This work brings dancers, thinkers and technologists into relation through rhythm and impact, exploring how we might move differently with time, technology and one another. It carries forward the same principles that shaped this book—impact as intelligence, feeling as method and imagination as survival—into shared practice. Together, these efforts form a growing ecosystem of learning and making that seeks to return motion to meaning, and to remind us that the future is something we must once again learn to dance.

Impact-driven dance—the subject of this study, and also a field of movement which Irish step dance weaves through—explores the intimacy of violences perpetrated by oppressors. For a colonizer of land, technology or identity, oppression is distant: strategic, bureaucratic. For impact-driven dancers, oppression is felt acutely and chronically, emerging and hiding in dreams, hopes, love-making and labor. Whether the shocks go unnoticed or are assumed into our own self-perception, we have a choice in how we respond. In my study—from the patting of mothers on the soles of their children's feet in song, to the slapping of brooms and swords, to the marching steps toward freedom—our percussive dances have always helped us heal and find a way forward.

Despite what academia suggests, it is impossible to study what it means to be someone else–especially if that someone belongs to a group you do not. At best, we can describe what we have observed happen to others. We can, however, listen. Academia can catalog other people, or it can become a field where we come to know ourselves and our role in the world more deeply.

Dance is uniquely suited to this second possibility. It is a study of comings and goings, risings and fallings, stillness and violence, growth and decay. We have been dancing since life first stirred in the sea, when motion became memory and rhythm became survival—long before we walked the earth in search of belonging. Dance endures not because it resists capture, but because it teaches continuation: how to stay in motion when everything else stops.

As long as we are here, dance—more than any other art form, including books, music, or architecture—will be with us. It is not simply an art, but the pattern through which life remembers itself. If, for you, dance has been only momentary or "other," that is fine—it will still find you. But if you have ever tapped your feet to re-regulate your nervous system after trauma, pounded your chest after heartbreak, or clapped your hands for truth—and you would like to make that movement your way forward—each step is a small act of decolonizing destiny. This book is for you.

Russell Patrick Brown PhD

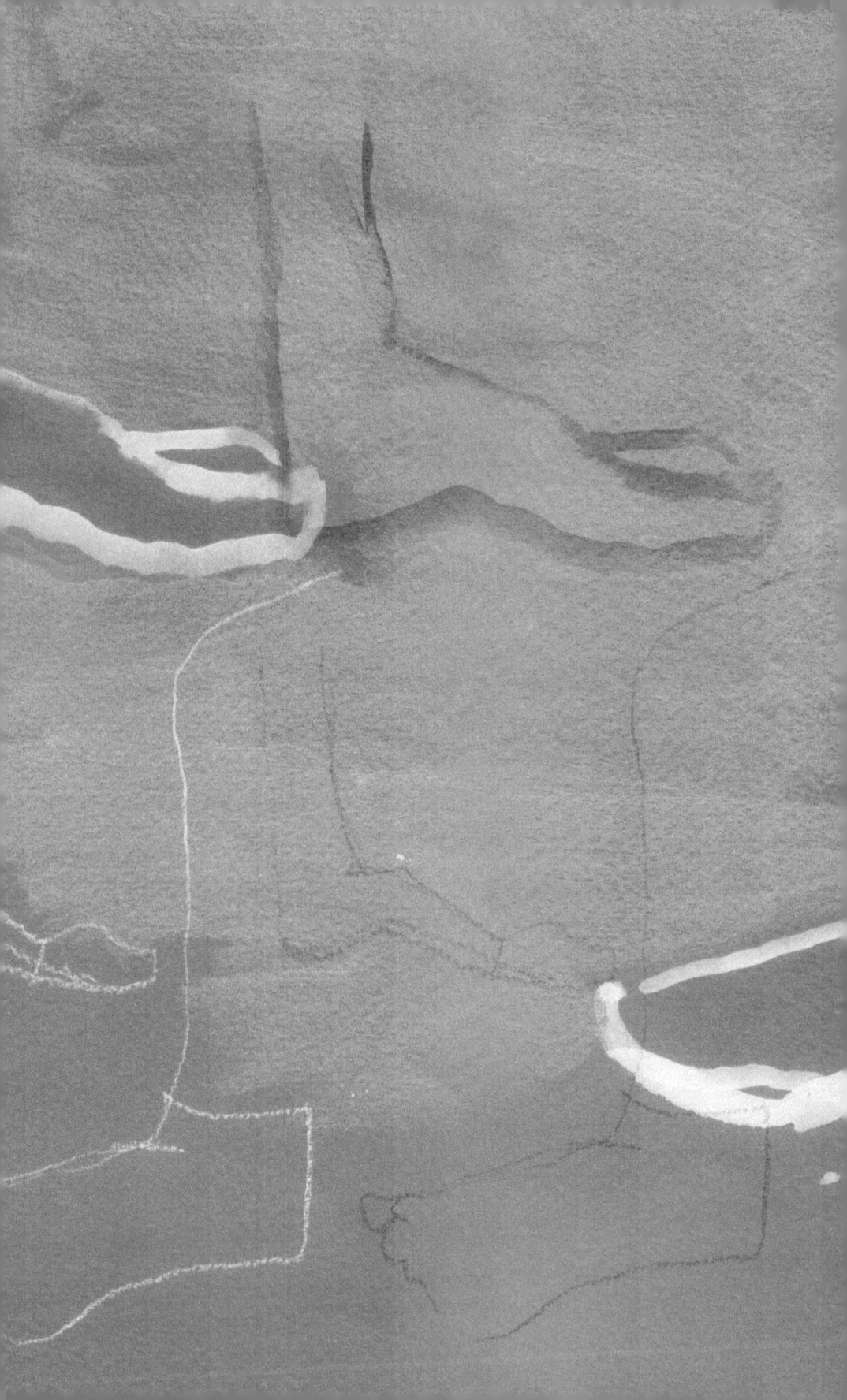

Timedancers: Feeling Impact in Irish Step Dance

Abstract

Timedancers: Feeling Impact in Irish Step Dance takes an Arts Practice approach to traditional Irish step dance and early dance research. I use a psychometric (object-reading) theoretical perspective so that we can learn more about the somatic experience of both material and immaterial objects and phenomena in the formation and evolution of impact-driven dance. Great strides have been made to unpack the complex legacies and practices of percussive dances such as Tap, Flamenco and Ballet Folklorico, especially from the perspectives of race, class and the role of nationalism in shaping memory and tradition. These studies have primarily relied on visual, auditory and kinetic interpretations of percussive dance that leave room for more study of the somatic, felt experience of percussive dance history and practice. An Arts Practice methodology mobilizes my processes as an Irish traditional step dancer and dance historian working in the 17th- and 18th-century Atlantic world. I theorize, document and use dance itself as a means to carry out this research. This project draws on the experience of a lifelong, intergenerational impact-driven dancer who became a western academic researcher over the past decade. With some assistance from autoethnography, personal narrative and mind-mapping my theoretical perspective, the thesis develops a post-human performative (Barad 2003) understanding of my identity as a Queer, Romani cisgender male living with disabilities, performing and researching Irish traditional step dance. Each piece of my identity contributed to a psychometric theory that has provided insight into fashions, societal structures, gestures and meanings within Irish step dance.

"The Querist", Or, Questions Posed By A Contemporary "Travelling Dance Master" was my first theatrical representation of this research, performed in 2017 at the University of Limerick Irish World Academy of Music and Dance. In this performance, I used psychometrical studies of dance manuals, high heels, gloves and important phenomena to explore the development of Irish step dance and dance more broadly in the 18th century. My second major output, *AngelAI*, performed in 2023 in the same location, focused on the objects and enduring phenomena of violence, colonization and oppression I encountered personally and/or witnessed happening to others past or present during a five-year hiatus from formal doctoral study. In this case, psychometry affirmed that my dance was not just an exploration of the optic, sonic or kinetic, but was more a haptic dance of impact felt most acutely in the moment of contact between foot and ground before anything is seen, heard or interpreted. Storytelling and academic writing re-traces this journey from the intuitive knowledge of objects in the history of dance to discovering an impact-driven dance fluent in the material, economic and prejudiced disruptions and intimate violence of our ever-evolving post/colonial world.

Acknowledgements

As eleven years of academic research and forty years of Irish step dancing in the United States and Ireland come to a close and new chapters begin, I give thanks to those who have helped me put all the steps together. I also acknowledge and give thanks to the lands in which I have lived and taken these steps, and to the people who have cared for them since time immemorial. I give thanks to the Lenape and their unceded ancestral lands of Lenapehoking, and to the long-held African-American and Romani refuge that is the Greenwich Village of Manhattan. I also give thanks to the many Native Americans whose lands my family's Romani caravans have traveled over since the 1800s, from the Erie in Northeast Ohio to the Cherokee in Georgia. I give thanks to Irish people who have so often welcomed me back to Ireland, and the Estonians who have protected their lands and language for thousands of years and welcomed me there to dance.

I would like to thank Breandán de Gallaí, my supervisor, for believing in me from the beginning of this doctoral journey and always guiding me back to myself, unreservedly. Thank you also to my original supervisor, Catherine E. Foley, for agreeing to take on my wild vision in the first place and always asking the best of me and my research. Thank you to my editors and reviewers for your patience and guidance with this research. Thank you to Helen Phelan for creating the incredible Arts Practice PhD, which challenged me to actually do what I say I am doing. Thank you also to Niamh NicGhabhann for welcoming me into the Festive Arts MA program so that I could better learn the languages of encounter. Thank you Eoin Callery for supporting the technological twists to my research in the last few years and to Orfhlaith Ní Bhriain, Mats Melin, Mary Nunan, Mary Wycherly, Jennie Roche and Grant McLay for creating a haven for Irish dance at the Irish World Academy and for many encouraging conversations as I found my footing in the dance world. Thank you to Colin Dunne for helping me with housing and dance chats in my first year in Limerick. Thank you also to Alan Dormer and the technical teams at IWA for making my dance productions possible, and thanks to all the faculty and staff of the IWA for helping me with the countless requests and chats this project required, including helping me when I showed up on my first day of school with all my bags and no place to live. Thank you also to Hannah Santino, Hala Jaber, Mary McLaughlin, Eli Painter, Aimee McKenzie, RAS Mikey Courtney and the many wonderful classmates in various degree programs who truly made the Academy a home and always welcomed me back. Special thanks to Sandra Joyce, Niall Keegan and Mel Mercier for helping me through the hard parts and always offering whatever assistance I needed. Lastly, a deep thanks to Mícheál Ó Súilleabháin for creating the Academy and so warmly welcoming me to it.

At New York University, thank you to my supervisor John Waters for pointing me in the direction of Irish dance research and to my thesis advisor Daniel Neely for helping me write my master's thesis, which was the seedbed of this project. Thank you also to Mick Moloney for encouraging me to continue my research at the doctoral level and for pioneering so much research on Irish-American music and dance with Lenwood Sloan, and so generously enlightening us all with it. Thank you to Jean Butler for giving me my first guest lecture opportunity and for introducing me to practice-based research in Irish dance. Thank you also to Miriam Nyhan for being a cheerleader from the beginning and to all the faculty at Glucksman Ireland House who introduced me to academia. Thank you also to the Performance Studies Department for expanding my education and to Seán Curran and the Tisch Department of Dance for a magical month-long residency that helped me bring my dance research home to New York from Ireland.

Thank you to Finola Cronin and the University College Dublin School of English, Drama and Film for providing me with a residency and invaluable mentorship on choreographing for the stage. Thank you also to Paul Halferty and Cormac O'Brien for nurturing my queer sensibilities in research and to Victoria Secret and the Dublin Drag Queens for even now still keeping me as a part of your magical, rigorous world. Thank you also to Iveagh Fitness for being so generous and encouraging with my dance research and training regimen. Thank you also to Declan English for always letting me wander into your shop and vent, and for your visual artistry (including TMNJ), your dinners with Breandán and for the very many laughs. You taught me not to take myself too seriously, which you knew I would do anyway.

In Galway, thank you Rachel Parry for countless talks on dance research, and for introducing me to the wonderful dancers, actors and staff of Speckled Egg Dance Company and the Blue Teapot Theatre Company, whose expertise greatly influenced the trajectory of my research. Thank you also to Genevieve Ryan, Galway Dance Project, Kiki St Clair, Martin & Club GASS and Louis de Paor for the many wonderful adventures dancing in your wonderful city. In Limerick thank you to *mo bhean an tí*, Ailish Barry, for always providing me, my cards and my harp at home in Limerick and encouraging me to finish my studies. Thank you also to the gang at Stroker's, our after-hours queer singer sessions were a complete education.

In Estonia, thank you to Evelyn and John Grzinich and the community at MoKS for a transformative residency. In England, thank you to my dear friends Cheryl Kelley and Phil Burns for being part of my academic journey from the beginning and many excited phone calls after each major discovery. Thank you to Sarah Whatley at the University of Coventry C-DaRE for fielding so many questions on dance research. Thank you to my mediumship mentor, Mavis Pittilla, and to Jean Else for helping me understand the spirit in my body and how to demonstrate our connection to the divine.

In Clare, many thanks to the Lahinch Leisure Centre for providing essential training grounds, and to the Burren Artist

Studios for precious studio time to develop my work. Thank you also Daire Skuce, Jackie Askew and the dance community of Ennistymon for helping me find the dance of daily life. To Maria Kerin and Michael Walsh, your friendship, inspiration and drinks by the fire warmed my journey on its darkest nights, and Maria without you this project simply would not exist. To this community that has welcomed me so many times, you are the impact in my Irish step dance, and you always inspire me with your compassion for the victims of war in Ukraine, Palestine, Sudan, Israel and around the world.

Thank you to my *kumpania*, Rosamaria Kostic Cisneros, Piroska Racz, El Rubito de Granada, Dezso Mate, Cristiana Grigore and many other Roma and Sinti scholars, activists and artists who have enriched my life. Piroska and Rubito, you have taught me what can never be taken away from us. Thank you also the European Roma Institute for Arts and Culture and Cristiana Grigore and the Columbia Roma People's Project for accepting me, teaching me and giving me a voice. Thank you also to Ann Ostendorf, Meira Golberg, Jacqueline Shea Murphy, Noémie Ndiaye, Lizzie Leopold and the Dance Studies Association for being allies, and Meira thank you for helping me find my writing voice.

In New York, thank you Kristina Varade for being a dear friend and taking every ridiculous call and question I had with patience and enthusiasm. Thank you Claire Conceison for always making the life of the academic seem more glamorous and inspiring than it so often is. May Joseph, you have been such an inspiration to me and your research opened my mind and my "fluid" sense of place in my performance in so many ways. Thank you to Donny Golden for teaching me to be the best Irish step dancer I could be. Thank you also to Niall O'Leary, Darrah Carr and Darrah Carr Dance for giving me my first Irish step dancing jobs when I moved to New York City. Thank you also to Brendan Fay, Kathleen D'Arcy Walsh, Malachy McCourt, Peter Quinn, Honor Molloy, Aidan Connolly and the good people of the Lavender and Green Alliance / St Pat's for All for creating such a special place for me begin to publicly be Irish-American and gay—and for winning marriage equality in not just one but two countries. Thank you also to all the people in New York City's cabaret, nightlife and performance art world for being the reason I moved to New York and teaching me how to be alone on stage. A very special thank you also to Maureen Fleming for sharing your many decades of wisdom, your magic for dance and teaching me about the life of the artist, and for training me in Fleming Elastxx. Thank you also to Chris Odo for the many wonderful meals, rides and incredible, patient videography and lighting. My deep gratitude to James Eden for helping guide me to healing after the initial outbreak of the pandemic, for nurturing the return of my spiritual life and teaching me about plant medicine. Thank you to Jacques Michaane for helping me fight to keep my home and Andrew Berman of Greenwich Village Preservation for always giving me good press and information. Thank you also to my dear friend Kira Citron for listening to me drone endlessly about whatever I needed to complain about and teaching me resilience.

Thank you to my friends Jon Murach and Michael Georgalis for teaching me the gentleness and friendship of men. Thank you to Brent Williams for helping me find my body again—twice. Thank you to Emilie Jabouin for our informal colloquium of ideas, hopes and dreams. To Amira Zayad, thank you for inspiring my dance of resistance and solidarity for the Roma from the Shoshone-Paiute and Palestine. Thank you to Patricia L. Bell for showing me how to be a researcher, dancer and spiritual practitioner, and a good friend. Thank you to my sister Colleen Brown Valdez and her husband Jose Valdez for all the love and for standing by me through all the hardship. Thank you to my father, Raymond Brown, my mother Laura Brown Franklin and my stepfather Denver Franklin for giving me a childhood rich in culture and guiding me to the power of hard work. Lastly, thank you to all my friends, family, colleagues, neighbors and all those who helped me on my journey. Thank you for the impact you have had on my life. I give impact-driven dance back to you.

Chapter One:

Introduction

In the 2016 film, *Arrival*, after aliens land in twelve ships throughout different parts of the globe (Villeneuve), the US military solicits the help of linguistics professor Dr Louise Banks to learn how to communicate with them. She discovers that the unique, annular language of the "heptapods" causes them to experience time completely differently from the way it is experienced in the linear languages of humans. Having learned the heptapods' language, she gains a new perception of life and becomes able to foresee all the blessings and tragedies that are to come, an ability that ultimately enables her to alter the fate of humanity and the heptapods alike. In the film, the extraterrestrials' language is symbolized by a circle with striations and accents, not unlike a coffee stain. This symbol captures the fact that those fluent in the heptapods' language acquire a non-linear, circular perspective on their lives and the wider world. Villeneuve's film raises myriad thoughts and questions. Among them for myself were: is my language holding back my own perception of my dance? In the times I have felt a more connected sense of past, present and future, was there some inner, embodied speech making this possible?

I revisited *Arrival* at the end of my research. At the beginning and in the final stages of this doctoral project, I suspected that I did not have the right way of thinking, at least in English, about my Irish step dancing practice within the greater, mysterious whole that is percussive dance. The academic intersection of history with tradition disturbed my dance. Something started to happen in practice, rehearsals and performances that I could not understand. The present thesis explores this process and strives to create a system of communication (primarily through English) that is capable of imparting this understanding to others. Impact-driven dance and all its intimate violences fold *kalipen* (darkness/time) into a *chakra* (wheel),[1] at once connecting and transcending trauma, creativity and humanity through the act of stomping on the earth.

Would you dance any differently if you already knew where you were going when you started? Would you dance tradition any differently if you assumed that your ancestors did not know full well what they were doing when they started? Maybe these questions are irrelevant for you, and in that case all I can offer is a journey through my own dance and research. When I began Irish step dancing, choreographing and researching, I neither knew what I was doing, nor did I believe my predecessors understood what they were doing when they created this dance form. If you have felt the same way, this project might interest you: impact-driven dance and all its intimate violences might help you to reconsider what has always been there in your dance as well as in our collective dance.

---

[1] I am referencing Romanes, the Romani language, with reference to some of its Sanskrit origins. This will be further explored throughout this dissertation.

Thesis Layout

I submit this work in fulfillment of the requirements of my PhD Arts Practice at the Irish World Academy of Music and Dance at the University of Limerick. My research began in September 2015, a few months after completing my Master's in Irish and Irish-American Studies at New York University's Glucksman Ireland House. I originally proposed to apply an Arts Practice approach to my research in Irish step dance and dance history in order to better understand the influence of 18th-century materialism on the development and practice of step dance in Ireland. My hope was not just to obtain a better understanding of the origins of Irish step dance, but to discover through history (academic) and tradition (lived) how we become and express ourselves with movement. Undertaking a practice-based methodology was a process of personal "becoming" (Obama 2018). Each chapter in this text presents a new identity, a title that I assumed to confront this task wholly and responsibly, in an embodied manner, conscious of the attendant power structures. Each persona revisits the same topics and themes in a spiral pattern, circling through time, tradition and trauma in an effort to go deeper as well as forward into the subject of impact-driven dance.

Chapter Two, *An Draoí* lays out my practice, explains my methodology and defines terms. Practice-informed academic research has for decades existed to facilitate reflexivity in knowledge production. I argue that, in many communities, dance has always combined research with practice. My "expert" (Melrose 2006) dance practice is my primary method of research. It was created in my life within my families and extended communities. My academic journey as a dance historian and later Arts Practice researcher has allowed me to interrogate my practice in many ways. Practice-informed research in dance has required me to become more familiar with contemporary dance, somatic practice and dance theater. This education has provided me with some critical faculties and allowed me to re-present my context-specific dance practice to a broader audience, although I have made no attempts to launch this work into the circuit of not-for-profit arts organizations and funding bodies. This is in part because I am primarily a folk harper, singer, storyteller and embodied technologist (I manage software engineers for a living) and dance is not something I choose for a living. Dance for me is a lifestyle that lives in a familial temporality (both genetic and chosen). I have only limited interactions with dance in a professional temporality.

My documentation of this practice is based on "autoethnographic cartography" (MacDonald 2016). This is informed by personal narrative, mind-mapping and video recording, which have allowed me to critically reflect on the capitalist, white patriarchal and colonial "new materialisms" (Barad 2003; Grosz 2010; et al.) arising through my choreography and research in early dance.[2] This process involved documenting and critically engaging with two "major works" I created to fulfill the requirements of this program. The first work was staged in September 2017 and, after a five-year hiatus from my doctoral studies, the second in November 2023. My documentation informs this mandated 40,000-word minimum dissertation, which forms a standalone complement to the creative dance pieces. All three works connect to one another, and strive to support hyperchronic somatic awareness in what can be called "percussive dance". By "hyperchronic somatics" I denote a heightened feeling or sense of all times in this time that can take place inside the body of an impact-driven dancer. This framework raises the question of who feels what within their dance and what dancers past and present are expected to feel in performance, especially when it comes to violent gestures that feature in major dance works. All of these considerations are specific to community, context, identity and other factors. Some of them can be expressed only in the choreographic portions of this work while others can be expressed only in writing. As this

---

2 "Early dance" is the term generally applied to the study of dance before 1800. It is preferred to the term dance history owing to the problematic colonial legacy of the discipline and, more broadly, history.

project is a first-person research project, I cannot claim to define this experience for others, but I do wish to acknowledge how they have helped me to bend time in my dance.

The beginning of each chapter contains autoethnographic cartography in the form of poetry inspired by the epic Irish Gaelic and Indian Sanskrit traditions, with some inspiration from the Griot and Kora player Salieu Suso.[3] Storytelling was at the center of my Irish-American and Romani upbringing, giving me a direct ancestral connection to epic oral storytelling forms and their "particular constellation of meaning that cannot be made known by any other means" (Smith and Fowle 2012: 30). Smith and Fowle refer here to theories of visual art curation, however their analysis of "encounter" also applies to epic poetry's ability to assemble verse, prose, myth, legend, annals, maps, genealogies, hagiographies and more into a single creative work. In the case of Ciaran Carson's *The Táin*, his translation of the Irish epic *Táin Bó Cúailnge*, these complex and often contentious works can be viewed holistically as "[…] a magnificently ruined cathedral, whose fabric displays the ravages of war, fashion and liturgical expediency: a compendium of architectural interpolations, erasures, deliberate archaisms, renovations and restorations; a space inhabited by many generations, each commenting on their predecessors" (Carson 2009: xiv). I do not wish to suggest that my thesis is comparable to the great epics of antiquity, only that it is an experiment in expressing my living connection to this tradition. These poetic passages translate the "ruined cathedral" I have inherited in impact-driven dance. The academic paraphrases that accompany these poetic passages are intended to show that storytelling makes knowledge known in a "constellation of meaning" that only it can reveal—exposing the inability of academic prose to capture what is best expressed creatively. Moreover, epic poems do not always tell a single epic tale, but rather constitute a system of overlapping stories that mix different

---

3   I had the privilege of collaborating with Salieu in the 2000s at the Bowery Poetry Club in New York City with producer and poet Christine Timm.

forms of verse as well as prose. They are evolving works that can in themselves be understood as forms of research with their own particular culturally specific methods.

The next main identity I inhabited within this doctoral project is *The Psychometrist*. She/he/they represent(s) my theoretical lens. I have consistently applied feminist new materialisms to the study of tangible and intangible objects and phenomena. This is a study of the post-human, of permeations between objects and events, actors and the acted upon. The feminist new materialist framework has allowed me to better grasp the conditions, societal structures, fashions and subcultures that have influenced the formation of Irish step dance throughout its history in local and global contexts. My Irish, Queer, Romani and Disabled identities have allowed me to use these theories to explore the legacies of violent materialisms visited on these people. These violent materialisms were typically perpetuated by white, cisgendered men—an identity to which I myself have access as I am white-passing and mostly cisgendered. In many contexts there exist anxieties around claiming and defining identities, especially as they relate to minoritized communities. My intention here is to use my experience as either a member, guest or outsider within these communities and to benefit from the knowledge they have shared with me, both as part of this project and beyond. Impact-driven dance is a dance of intimacy. I have found it too difficult to write without drawing on these identities—these lives—as acknowledged, present and further engaged in the asking of questions. The Psychometrist, a word with a few different meanings, is defined by the lens of "encounter" (Bourriaud 1998) turned on the site of the step dancer's fashions. This is a moment my friend, the dance artist Maria Kerin refers to as "dreaming into" before the task of becoming begins. As discussed in Chapter Four, *The Querist*, fashions mediate meetings of self and other and shape how we move through what is significant. Taking this approach to objects also takes on a mystical significance, and suggests an intent on the part of the Psychometrist: to know the history of an object through touch.

These two chapters conclude the AA of the AABB structure (common in Irish dance music) of this dissertation. The BB is formed by two major artistic works: *The Querist* and *AngelAI*. The first of these works—like my first two chapters—was not informed directly by violence as the revelation that violence was central to understandings of Irish dance did not happen until the second half of 2022 into 2023. In creating the second major work, *AngelAI*, the excavation of violence led to a surprising discovery of resilience, ingenuity, resistance, therapeutic benefit and even transcendence in impact-driven dance. Furthermore, I discovered that it was possible that the process of healing through choreography could awaken legacies of violence. As I moved, I realized that I was healing and I discovered from what it was I needed to be healed. Deeper still, I acquired a wholeness within my own expression of the tradition.

Considerations

These repeated collisions, whether healing, creative or nonsensical, have the potential to unveil a new understanding of the formation of step dance in the Atlantic world, one that goes beyond existing visual, auditory and sociological interpretations of the form. Dancing impact in this Arts Practice project has been to explore the history, practice and future of this form using the language of the body and the language of intimate violence. In the choreo-linguistics of impact-driven dance, intimate violence is defined as a collision of self and surface. Whether it be foot against floor, hand against fan or soul against society, there is impact that is felt individually—intimately. The causes of this violence may be colonial, racist, patriarchal, technological, anti-Gaelic or anti-gypsyist.[4] Regardless, they all symbolize interruption through disruption—to use a contemporary, much-lauded tech term expressing the capitalist drive to "move fast and break things" (i.e., move fast and take things that do not belong to you in the name of

---

[4] The word "gypsy" is a racial slur, and I do not capitalize its usage.

technological innovation). This project's analysis of the creation, evolution, subversion and re-enactment of intimate violences through dance builds a framework for advancing research into the violent histories of dance.

The past few decades of percussive dance scholarship have opened the art form to discussion of nationalism, race and community in addition to visual and sonic interpretations of the form. Although many problems and gaps remain, some shared insight is beginning to form. Studies in Tap dance have revealed worlds of feeling and conflict within the study of this African-American art form, its theory and history. As I have found in my scholarship on Flamenco—a Gitano, Roma, Calé and Zincailli dance form influenced by peoples and cultures from North African, Jewish, Arab and Andalusian communities—Romani voices are still marginalized and in most cases entirely excluded from the scholarship. The contribution of the Spanish Roma to the development of the art form is dismissed by non-Roma academics on grounds of unacknowledged anti-gypsyism and gadje-centrism (i.e., non-Roma-centrism).[5] I have learned that gadje generally do not understand how to be a guest within a dance culture, they only understand how to own something. In Gaeilge and *Romanes* there are no verbs that signify "to own"

---

5 As Flamenco has grown in popularity and reaped profits in the United States, it has become common for the gadje (non-Roma) to dismiss the role of the Roma in the history of the art form in order to secure professional performing opportunities. I have spent the last five years fighting this trend as a scholar, activist and artist, and I have accepted that we (the other five or so Romani dance scholars out there and I) have lost this war. I give no citations of gadje appropriation, theft and racist scholarship as it is not safe to do so given that I can and have faced professional consequences for calling people out.

something.⁶ This suggests not a lack of understanding of this fundamentally capitalist word but indicates instead a different value system. On the other hand, Anita Gonzalez's foundational work on Afro-Mexican dance challenged the "whitening" present in Amalia Hernández's Ballet Folklorico, bringing to light the richness of Mexican dance history (Gonzalez 2010), albeit many challenges still lie ahead in Mexican dance scholarship. Over a decade ago, Arts Practice research at the University of Limerick Irish World Academy invited more personal, creative explorations of Irish step dance. Moreover, Breandán de Gallaí's research into authentic identity beyond nationalism and the untapped creative potential of the form constituted a turn in the field of Irish traditional dance studies (2013). This is particularly meaningful as de Gallaí embraces his native Irish language, which is marginalized in many contexts in Irish dance. These along with many other contributions to the study of percussive dance have awakened my own hope as an Irish step dancer that I can remain aware of the moment before a tap, snap, clap or stomp can be seen, heard or interpreted—that I can meet myself in all our complexity as I collide. I keep my heart in the moment of touch.

As I have worked within this framework, I have realized its capacity as a tool for reclamation. When speaking of colonialism, racism and technologies of torture used in the early modern period to enforce a capitalist agenda—something the evolution of Irish step dance is absolutely connected to—it is vital to recognize that these forms of impact landed in some communities and not in others. This has implications for the conclusions we are able to draw. Jasmine Johnson observes that, when we find written

---

6   Gaeilge and Romanes are not my first language and I am not a linguist, so I am treading gently on this as a concept. These languages do not explicitly state "I own this", but instead state "this is at me", "this is with me", "this is on me" and other prepositional phrases. This, it could be argued, implies the same connotations of ownership and possession but with more nuance in denoting the relationship between owner and owned. Given the volume of colonial law written in the English language and the fact that Gaeilge and Romanes have no history of perpetrating colonialism, I feel this differentiation is a compelling point of exploration for future researchers.

descriptions of Afro-diasporic people dancing, we cannot assume that these people were consenting to dance (2020). The "positive stereotype" of the Romani or Irish Traveller performer is not always embraced by these communities (Dobai and Hopkins 2020). Something similar could perhaps be said with regard to the stereotype that Irish people love to dance jigs and reels. Many communities have an "ambivalence" (Johnson 2020) towards dance, and many people simply prefer to have nothing to do with it. We cannot assume that the blanket term "percussive dance" implies any sort of unanimous experience for all communities of dancers. As this PhD journeys from practice to the psychometry of objects to the dancing of these problems, I intend the framework of impact not to smooth over differences, as "percussive dance" so often does. Instead, this framework will enable me to grapple with the challenges of assessing lived experiences in dance research and—where it is welcome—to support the agency of impacted communities in the practice, history and profiting of percussive dance, while also recognizing their ingenuity and creativity. In my own practice this has meant beginning to understand as well as celebrating the Blackness and anti-colonialism of Irish step dance,[7] as well as the *kalipen* and indigeneity of my own identity as a Romani Irish step dancer. Impact-driven dance's intimate violences cite various impacted lineages. I hope that this research encourages more discussion on this topic. I also wish to recognize the individuals and communities who have done the work of moving dance, and not just those who have profited from it.

This work is influenced and informed by what I have learned from Black, Afro-diasporic, Asian, Jewish, Latinx, Palestinian and Indigenous dance scholars, colleagues and friends. Without the work of Noémie Ndiaye, Jacqueline Shea Murphy, Anita Gonzalez, Rodreguez King-Dorset, Catherine Foley, Meira Goldberg, Thomas DeFrantz and Brenda Dixon-Gottschild and many colleagues, mentors and friends in academia and dance alike, I am doubtful I ever could have begun the journey of

---

7   An extremely rich topic with many sources I hope to explore further.

de-colonizing my mind, understanding internalized racism, and critically probing whiteness. Most important of all, they have taught me to take pride in myself and the traditions I have inherited, while recognizing those I have not inherited directly. Methodologically, their work has taught me how to translate my lived experience and my archival method for a white, non-Roma Anglophone world. A regret in this project is that it did not delve further into Black Performance Theory (BPT) (DeFrantz and Gonzalez 2014) and other related and divergent strands of discourse and dance. I have recently been accepted as a member and contributor to the European Roma Institute for Arts and Culture, where my "wheel of time" (Jordan 2021) will expand to probe Critical Romani Studies, Premodern Critical Race Theory, BPT, anti-Romani racism, anti-gypsyism (or gypsyism as I simply call it), Romanipen and my nascent invocation of kalipen as it relates to darkness, blackness and temporality in Roma and Sinti culture.

I wish for this work to facilitate a dialogue between somatic-led contemporary dance and traditional Irish dance forms. Intimacy and impact can help to improve our understanding of the collisions between self and surface that take place in Irish step dance, and that took place in the formation of percussive dance as we know it today. It can also help us to understand the "silent" crashes and bangs happening to and emanating from dancers who are set about tasks other than those of the percussive dancer. Together we are, perhaps, united in rising to the impacts of our past, our present and our future. In an Irish Studies context, I hope that I may continue this research into the study of itinerant harpers and dancing masters alike in the 17th and 18th centuries. I also hope that once this is complete I can finally spend more time improving my Gaeilge and Romanes!

This project began as an attempt to understand early Irish step dance, and became for me not just a new way of stepping Irish dance, but a new way of being an Irish step dancer. It is my greatest wish that my experience will encourage more people to explore Irish step dance and to make dances of impact that reveal new and unique ways of dancing in place. It may transpire that some of our greatest breakthroughs today will not involve new technologies that end up controlling our bodies, but ways of dancing capable of resisting these violences in this time and all times.

A Timedancer's Study of Irish Step Dance

Chapter Two:

An Draoí

[A jig, right foot in front]
Jump, kick, hop back-234
Jump, kick, hop back-234
Jump, kick, hop back-234
Hop, hop back, hop back-234

In this chapter, I introduce my practice as an Irish step dancer and dance historian in greater detail. I also explain the Arts Practice methodology that I will be using to answer my research questions. Practice-based research, Irish step dance and dance history each have complex histories, and so my definition of these terms will have a significant bearing on my findings.

Outside the present research, I have a varied practice as an artist, scholar and technologist. Moreover, the way in which I relate to and identify with these roles is complex. During the early stage of this research, I struggled to understand how these parts of my practice fit together and how they inform my study of historical materialism and Irish step dance. In the later phase of the project, this problem diminished as I came to realize that these facets of my practice are not in fact the principal subject of this study. Nevertheless, some parts of my identity and broader artistic and spiritual practice have shaped my approach to the study of Irish step dance and dance history. I will consider this in greater detail in the next chapter where I introduce the project's theoretical framework.

The present chapter, meanwhile, will introduce what Arts Practice is, what methodology I will use and how I define key terms and theories. Practice-based research is still a fairly novel phenomenon in academia outside conservatory degrees such as the Master of Fine Arts. The process of academic research can, of course, be viewed as a kind of practice in itself. However, by practice-based research I refer here specifically to doctoral study in the arts where practicing the artform that one studies forms part of the research and output. In my country of origin, the United States, practice-based research is still forbidden to doctoral candidates in the arts and humanities. My participation in two different academic systems (the US/North America and Ireland/Europe) informs my definition of Arts Practice research. I obtained my baccalaureate and master's degree under the American system, while this doctoral project has been carried out within the European system, which nurtures a small practice-based research community. It is my hope this research has been strengthened by the influence of both systems, straddling them logistically and theoretically. My experience of studying under American and European systems has given rise to one of the core findings of this project, namely that impact-driven dancers are often engaged in a dance with authority and that the logic of that authority is as active today as it was in the early modern Atlantic world. When considered from a colonial perspective, the issue of the legitimacy of different knowledge-systems is an old one. In what follows, I will argue that this distinction is less about legitimacy and more about legibility to the colonial gaze, particularly when it comes to addressing the meaning of impact-driven dance in different contexts and the way their exercise constructs time.

This chapter draws on the principle of *An Draoí*. This is an Irish language word with multiple meanings and captures the first major "identity" that I will draw on. The word has four meanings which I will use to shed light on the topics discussed in this chapter: trickster (self & practice), druid (Arts Practice research), magician (methodology) and augur (theoretical terms).

The Trickster: Situating Self & Practice

For a short time in my life I did not
Dance alone. The wooden ceiling, columns,
Disco ball of Die Deutsche Zentrale[8]
In Parma, Ohio spun as dad waltzed,
Holding me in his arms across the floor.

East Side, West Side Irish-American
Clubs called us to music, meals, crafts, games,
The seanchaí fed us Gaeilge and tales.
At night the old dance hall swelled for céilí,
With twice as many watching from the porch.

This was no boring night of folk dancing!
The sunset shouted the names of dances:
"The Siege of Ennis", "The Stacks of Barley",
"The Highland Fling." Precision, formation:
The floor heaved and the crowd began to move.

Amidst flirtation and fist-fights a child
Learns advances, cuts, crosses, baskets that
Appear and dissolve in the July air.
Is this the movement of the heavens?

---

8 "The German Central" was built in 1924 to be a "home away from home" for the growing population of German-American Cleveland suburbanites, see History of German Central 2015.

Paraphrase

When I was a child, dance was not something to do alone on the dance floor, it was something to do as a community. To dance Irish traditional social dances was to be lifted by your loved ones across the room in the musical arms of a live band made up of those you have known since birth. At no time in my childhood did I feel this enchantment more strongly than at the German Central Fairgrounds. The Irish-American community rented the dance hall's fairgrounds once a year for a long weekend. A joint effort by the East Side and West Side Irish-American clubs, this magical summer weekend featured live music, arts, crafts, Gaelic games, home-made food and storytelling for the children from County Kerry seanchaí, Batt Burns. On Friday and Saturday nights, the dance hall would swell with hundreds of céilí dancers. As soon as the céilí band began to play with the precision of a military drill everyone entered formation and the dance would begin. I knew the waltz and most of the easier group dances by the time I was three or four. However, my mother, father and older sister had to sneak me onto the dance floor because this experience was not for children; this was nightlife.

When my mother and father separated little by little, the joy that had accompanied the Irish-American part of my childhood faded into the bright, digital and commercial life of the 1990s suburban America. My family went to the East Side and West Side clubs less and less. Solo step dancing lessons stopped and we became a less and less familiar sight at The German Central. Dance, which was the only thing I could do well (or at all it seemed) as a child, disappeared from my curriculum and was replaced by baseball bench warming, movie nights watching other people dance and saxophone lessons. As *Riverdance* and its Celtic Tiger cocaine-fueled fabulousness brought greater popularity to Irish-American festivals in the mid-90s, the summer festival left The German Central and was held at the much larger Cuyahoga County Fairgrounds. An intimate pay-to-be-part-of-something weekend became an over-attended pay-to-watch-something commercial venture. As large touring acts thundered onto stage and Irish step dancers arrived sporting neon, sequined costumes and dancing to pre-recorded pop-inflected Irish traditional music, members of the old community hosted a céilí in a small hall in the rear of the fairgrounds. Only a dozen or so people showed up and the event was canceled. The nights dancing among the stars were over.

I spent some very awkward adolescent years as if I were a cryogenically-thawed freak who only knew how to do dances that had been dead for over a century. I learned how to do the popular 20th-century dances white Americans were doing (typically appropriated from people of color [POC]) at weddings and school dances. Then in high school I learned how to tap, swing and jazz dance in high school musicals. The trend was clear to me: the world of weekly social dancing I had grown up with became the occasional lonely dance to someone else's lonely pop song, while staring at other people's lonely dances at school functions, weddings and, later, nightclubs. Touch would become only a preview to sex. On stage, that rush of connection I felt as a child in progressional folk dance sometimes filled my heart, but it always left me empty and needing more. It was intimacy for sale. My family's Romani musical traditions helped to sustain me creatively during this time, as we upheld a common tradition in Romani families of visiting local cultural festivals and learning from other communities. It was enriching and thrilling at times, but very confusing for my sense of self as a dancer.

When I was twenty-two, I moved to New York City and realized it was time to return to Irish step dancing. Since then I have met lifelong friends, learned dances worthy to compete in the World Championships of Irish Dance in 2007 and 2008, undertaken professional work as an Irish step dancer and improvised steps for my own harp concerts until 2014.[9] There is one thing, however, that I still secretly longed for that I have never been able to rediscover: the experience of holding hands and

---

9   I have begun performing in concert again.

frantically grabbing a stranger's waist for a spin amidst laughter, sweat and the embrace of community.

The Storyteller

By introducing myself as an Irish step dancer and my experience with loneliness in dance, I seek to showcase my practice as a storyteller and dance historian. Storytelling comes to me from the seanchaí and other storytellers I grew up with, as well as from my Romani family where music, song and storytelling were practiced in the home, particularly in the kitchen. My affinity for epic poetry derives from this experience. Academically, I situate myself as a historian specializing in dance and the intersection of body with technology, be it fashion, industry, digital platforms or societal structures.

I am motivated to study the historical imbrication of technology and the body because I have found that it is often neglected in studies of the evolution of dance and embodiment. I view my academic practice as an opportunity to understand—and to feel—how the way we use technology makes us who we are. Historical human–technological encounters (HTEs) have rippling effects across time and space. Demonstrating the utility of the HTE framework, Thomas DeFrantz has studied blackface as technology, considering not just its problematic history, but also what the practice of white people painting their faces black enabled them to do in performance (2022). In American contexts, blackface minstrelsy was typically the province of first- and second-generation Irish immigrants seeking a foothold in the new economy (Moloney 2006). Irish-American blackface minstrelsy would spawn a lineage that ultimately gave rise to American musical theater, beginning with the minstrel-troupe music of David Foster and the early musicals of Harrigan, Hart and Braham (Moloney and Harrington 2009). As Mick Moloney observed in his decades of collaborative work with dancer, choreographer and historian Lenwood Sloan, when the first American blackface minstrel troops came to Ireland in the 1830s (Riach 1973), they brought with them the banjo. The banjo was played exclusively in Traveller communities for more than a century until the Irish trad movements of the 1950s grew its popularity ("The Lyric Feature: Common Ground" 2020). William Henry Lane "Master Juba" visited Ireland during *An Gorta Mór* ("the great hunger" or potato famine of 1845-1852) in 1849, though the history of his visit has yet to be studied. A discussion of technology and blackface does not (and should not) minimize or alleviate the cruelty of what blackface minstrelsy represents or its rationalization of racism. However, it can help us to study the many permutations of this art form, the motivations and techniques of its performers and the long afterlife of blackface aesthetics. Applying blackface as a technological framework has also been helpful in other colonial contexts. Consider, for example, the Irish novelist Maria Edgeworth's 19th-century "linguistic blackface", which stereotyped native Irish people for the entertainment of English and Anglo-Irish readers (Egenolf 2005). In this study of intimate violence as it relates to HTEs, I am interested in how marginalized communities have responded to, subverted and overcome these interactions to form new ways of being within, outside or in addition to these systems. In summary, I wish to show how technology has enabled us to move the way we do, not just by considering my own position, but the position of all of us who belong to this history.

My passion for study of the past and all its secrets blossomed as I learned about new methods in historiography: digital archives such as Eighteenth Century Collections Online,[10] revisionist history that allows us to critically engage with the past, Pre-modern Critical Race Studies and the collection and analysis of large historical datasets. These and other new tools that allow us to

---

10 Eighteenth Century Collections Online (ECCO) is a collaborative project across universities, libraries and institutions to catalogue and make digitally available over 180,000 titles published in the United Kingdom in the years 1701–1800.

consider the past holistically opens dance historiography to new sources and perspectives. To study the dances of centuries past may seem a fruitless or at least a limited endeavor. However, the dance between here and there, now and then is not diminished by these challenges but made stronger by them. New discoveries make our methodology more robust. The potential of education through cross-cultural understanding applies not just to the present, but to all times. It is hyperchronic. Our ability to trace our past corresponds to our ability to imagine new futures. Ultimately, what are we willing to ask of dance? What can dance research tell us about ourselves?

When it comes to my own dance history, I take little for granted. I do not assume that contemporary challenges to tradition are unprecedented. Rather, I believe them to be connected to another tradition: that of capitalism. The loss of Irish traditional folk dance that I experienced as a young dancer in Ohio represented a loss of community, physical touch and a shared sense of place. Family turmoil and capitalist alienation are not unique to my experience. Realizing this helped me to understand how impact-driven dancers were isolated by slavery, expropriation and the destruction of their communities.

In the last decade more attention has been given to loneliness as a public health issue. During the COVID global pandemic, it mounted to a public health crisis. From the effects of cyberbullying to life post physical trauma to self-isolation during a plague, loneliness as a form of traumatic stress is a serious contemporary dilemma, a topic ripe for studies in solo performance. Given the complex and often brutal history of the Atlantic slave trade, more attention in early dance and traditional dance studies should be given to the effects of isolation, alienation and confinement. When speaking of the slave auction block, Joseph Roach notes that:

> […] here resides a plausible, if as yet relatively unexplored, genealogy of performance. With music, dance and seminudity, the slave auction, as a performance genre, might be said to have

anticipated the development of the American musical comedy. It certainly had important linkages to the blackfaced minstrel show, which enacted the effacement of the cultural traditions of those of those whose very flesh signified its availability for display and consumption. (Roach 1996: 214–15)

Nineteenth-century drama incorporated the public spectacle of the auction block and the erotic fantasy it provided for slavers and white spectators alike (Ibid.: 220). In Eastern Europe the aesthetics of inhumanity reach far back to the 14th century with the experience of Roma slavery that, similar to African slavery, also has implications for our study of solo dance history.

The politics of isolation in solo performance are more substantial than has previously been appreciated. They evolved in popular culture in shocking ways, such as in the case of the English nobleman who danced "a hornpipe in fetters" (Bratton 1990), wearing manacles connecting wrists and ankles. Wooden shoes—like fetters—were associated with slavery, signifying poverty, oppression and deprivation/isolation (Brown 2022). They also were a symbol of theft of the natural world (forests) and refinement by colonists into a prime commodity (wood). The clattering of these shoes would suggest that the wearer has greater wealth than those who go barefoot but less than those who could afford multiple forms of footwear, including leather footwear. The next chapters will dive into the broader contexts and meaning of these technologies in impact-driven dance. Suffice it to say for now that once we lift the veil of nationalism from traditional dance forms, it becomes clear that we have only begun to appreciate their richness.

If humanity, or at least the white western world, has journeyed from dancing together to dancing apart (to not at all), it is incumbent on dance scholarship to understand why. The difference between dancing together and dancing apart is easy to take for granted in the case of Irish set or céilí dances[11] versus

---

11 I refer to two different types of group dancing common in Irish traditional folk dancing.

traditional solo dances. Dance history offers some insight into how social dances like the quadrille earned their popularity during the age of revolutions when self-motivated aristocratic decadence fell out of favor. This offers one potential context for understanding the evolution of social dances, and there are many more. The phenomenon of dancing alone, whether at the 17th-century French court or when "dancing for eels" in New York's Catherine Street Wharf in the 19th century, is the first intimate violence I wish to take into consideration. While isolation represents neither the worst of capitalism's cruelties nor the worst traumas of my life, it nevertheless connects directly to the universal plight of the impact-driven dancer: the fact that he is alone in his dance. This realization has haunted me, transforming my image of gleeful group choreographies into a tragedy of many people dancing alone in unison. This intimate violence embodies the societal machinations that isolate the dancer. The self is reduced to a body alone before others with only its flesh, its fashions and the floor to touch. It is this impact that thereby becomes the site of dance.

The definition of An Draoí as "trickster" also represents myself, the dancer, who whether by force or will—or a combination of the two—strives to prevail under capitalism. In my chapter, "'This Little Wooden World': Choreo-Navigating Maritime Dance" (Brown 2022) I discuss the precarious embodiment of maritime dancers navigating class and race in the Atlantic world via footwear: whether the wooden shoes of slaves, the abject poverty signified by bare feet, or the fine footwear of balletic court dancers. In this article, I argue that the maritime dancer's task was (and still is) to "choreonavigate" this fraught corporeal terrain and to find their way through it, even if their shoes have been muffled by rubber. This intervention was intended to be anti-colonial, anti-racist and anti-patriarchal and formed part of an edited volume on the history of Flamenco. My argument was that maritime dances, which can be categorized among percussive dances, constituted a kind of autoethnographic map of the embodied landscape of the early modern era. I attempted to understand the history of these dances without recourse to ethnic nationalist narratives of their evolution and to restore their creative impulses. This meant moving away from the temporality of dance commercialism (quick, disposable) to a personal, communal timelessness (enduring, evolving). I find it a challenge to enter into the complex and often paradoxical state of mind required to exist under twenty-first century capitalism. Nevertheless, I feel that dance always knows the way, even when our most precious moments with family and friends are monetized through social media and our creative essence is sucked into the maw of Artificial Intelligence. Our mere existence and the mere thought of resistance seem to open up new capitalist frontiers for exploitation. In this project I ask, how do we dance this problem? How do impact-driven dancers, like the maritime dancers of the early modern period, choreonavigate? How is privilege or the lack of it negotiated in gesture? As we feel like tricksters in a fraught system, how do we live ethically and morally?

At the intersection of my practice as an Irish traditional step dancer and my practice as a historian specializing in dance and 18th-century materialism, I attempt to connect the past to our present. To many scholars of early dance, this may appear to be a risky endeavor, something historiographically inadvisable that only a fraud or trickster would do. Others, given the horrors in the historical record, feel the past is best left in the past. I unreservedly own that the connection between tradition and history is the subject of my dance research. I not only recognize the practices that have never died out (Roach 1996: xii), but also the communities that have resisted their erasure, supported their evolution and that continue to guide our way. I also hope that this research prompts dance historians to question their own relationship to tradition. The loss of a tradition and the broader loss of indigeneity are byproducts of the colonial project which should be questioned on their own terms so as to better understand our biases. We are more likely to disbelieve the legitimacy of another's traditions when we think we have none of our own. Furthermore, impact-driven dance's relationship to intimate violence problematizes the view that systemic violence, physical torture and technologies of control are things of the past. These violences are perpetuated continually—including through ingested, microscopic technologies such as hormones, medications and even computers (Preciado 2013). They form part of the tradition of empire and remain intimate for perpetrators and victims alike long after the initial strike has occurred. Impact-driven dance enables the continual exploration of the intimate violence of violence itself, both temporally and atemporally.

In my dance and my research I often return to the memory of dancing in the kitchen with my mother and my father waking me up for school every morning playing the Irish tin whistle. Thus, I carry with me a culture of unbroken intergenerational somatic intimacy. I also return to my family's Romani tradition of connecting with local communities different from our own and learning from them with the guidance of Romani values systems. I have "solved" the problem of choreonavigating capitalism in the way my Romani ancestors have: working a technical trade and preserving music and the dance for yourself, your community and others in the odd gig. I also maintain an Irish-sense of concern and action for the rights of those who are oppressed. From this I have come to realize that even when I dance alone, they and all that came before them are dancing with me.

As An Draoí has invited in the trickster, I recognize the challenge of telling one's own story and the deception of memory as I attempt to situate my dance and my research. I also point to the dancer (myself) who must choreonavigate the problems of modernity by making himself into a trickster, someone who subverts, plays with, benefits from and re-invents a system. Both of these problems are evidence of another problem in research: how objectivity and authority are defined in the academy. The next section on Arts Practice methodology discusses the trustworthiness of narrators, academic or otherwise, in greater detail.

The Druid: Entering an Arts Practice Tradition

Prior to my move to Ireland in the fall of 2015, I was not aware that practice-based research could exist within academia. As someone who has spent a life steeped in movement practices that are intertwined with knowledge-systems, and communities, the premise of practice-informed research—that doing and thinking should be connected—was familiar to me. In 2020, Orfhlaith Ní Bhriain argued before the *Oireachtas* for the Irish government to support all forms of dance, and to continue to support "thinking dancers" through education (Sexton 2020). This has been an important lesson from my time in Irish traditional dance culture, including when competing as part of *An Coimisiún Le Rincí Gaelacha* (the Irish Dancing Commission). However, I did not know that it was possible to advance this position in my scholarly research through dance itself. In my experience in American academia, it was impossible for practice to be my primary method of research and dissemination and impossible to conceive of how it ever could be. In New York's artistic and academic circles, institutions and their funding are established in a way that forbids practice and research from intersecting. As a result of dualism during my master's degree at New York University, my body ritualized superhero-esque transformations between the scholar and the creative self. By the time I was ready to depart to Limerick for my Arts Practice program, I knew of no viable option to unite, undermine or transcend this duality for an academic audience, nor did those around me. The problem was formulated by a NYU Performance Studies professor who said to the class, "the [academic] job is writing. Anyone who tells you otherwise is deceiving you."

The task of overcoming this invisible schism is critical not only to understanding Arts Practice research, but also to understanding why it remains unintelligible to the seemingly un-embodied or body-less minds of so many academics. In my first year of studies at the Irish World Academy, Arts Practice research re-affirmed for me that the body and its experiences are vital and inseparable from my mind. Cognitive linguists and scientists George Lakoff and Mark Johnson have written that, "the mind is not merely embodied, but embodied in such a way that our conceptual systems draw largely on the commonalities of our bodies and the environments we live in" (Lakoff and Johnson 2008: Kindle locations 93–95). From these initial readings a question occurred to me: how can I hold this objective American academic tradition (it is certainly not just American but in my story it predominately is) alongside this Irish Arts Practice tradition that called forward personal traditions I had hidden from the academy? The way forward would be pointed by others.

To an Otherworld: Entering a Liminal Discipline

When attending the Irish World Academy's 2015 *Samhain* presentations, an annual autumn symposium for the department featuring doctoral presentations, my still-uprooted American academic alter-ego mentally annihilated most of the presenter's arguments. To my positivist academic mind, the research did not demonstrate the types of authority to which I was accustomed. While I respected the faculty's rigorous enquiry into the depth, relevance and standard of the research, I felt we were inhabiting two different worlds. My body did, however, register what was at times an almost eerie atmosphere in the room caused by the PowerPoint portals opened by the Irish researchers. As I have come to learn thanks to Robin Nelson's comprehensive study of practice-based research, this experience occurred because I was encountering research that did not just present new knowledge, but new types of knowledge that were almost incomprehensible to someone of my prior academic training (Nelson 2013: 31). If a body of knowledge is truly new to us, the way to experience it will also be new and difficult to contextualize, if not near impossible to witness. To understand is to be transformed, and to be transformed is to understand.

As a dancer I have been described as fairy-like, not just for my queerness but for the connection to the Otherworlds I experience when I dance. My early years on the Arts Practice program involved an awkward, staggered, ogre-like metamorphosis. Brute attempts to do what I was thinking and to think what I was doing felt dishonest and betrayed the previous faith I had had in my dance. A scholar speaking at the university-hosted Irish Traditional Song Symposium on "Song as a Liminal Play Sphere: Aesthetics and Ideas/Taireachúlacht agus Imeartas na hAmhránaíochta: an Aeistéitic agus an Machnamh" (Ní Shíocháin 2015) highlighted a new path of knowing for me. The scholar, Tríona Ní Shíocháin, had discovered the liminal nature of the imagined place that traditional Irish artists and their art so often drift towards. While singing, the *amhránaí* will stand between our world and the Otherworld, creating a liminal space (McLaughlin 2015). I was brought back to seanchaí Batt Burn's Irish lessons and forward to a journey between the dogged American academic and the Irish Arts Practice academic. I cite this transitional link to an Otherworld to explain the bridge between academic research and artistic practice. I do not define what is the Otherworld and what is the "real" world, but rather adopt a particular application of liminality for my own process of working between dance and text, theory and practice, impact and reflection.

The smells of embodied, artistic and transformative ways of knowing have lingered long. Evidence abounds in ancient but extant practices originating in East Asia like Yoga and Tai Chi.[12] In the Black, Indigenous and Romani communities I grew up among in Cleveland, embodied knowledge-systems have similarly endured uninterrupted (although certainly challenged) for thousands of years. Nevertheless, they remain marginalized in academia due the influence of gypsyism, racism and colonialism. As Lakoff and Johnson observe, the techniques of empire have sought over the last 2,000 years to accomplish the impossible: to subtract thought from body. The success of this illusion is reflected in the metaphors of common language. During the early modern period René Descartes, a seminal figure of emergence of modern philosophy and science, often used in his writing "the commonplace Knowing Is Seeing metaphor" (Lakoff and Johnson 2008: Kindle Location 4872). The very term "enlightenment", furthermore, suggests that the knowledge obtained by western philosophers at this time brought light into the world after a period of darkness. Even though vision certainly comes from the body, sight is closely connected to the mind and to earlier Christian thought, echoing the idea of Jesus as the light of the world and of pagans living in abyssal darkness and sin. Richard Shusterman's *Body Consciousness: A Philosophy of Mindfulness*

---

12 Tai Chi was built into the taught lectures of my doctoral program. Our Tai Chi class was usually placed in the middle of our immersion contact weeks, and it surprised me how much it disrupted, irritated and yet nourished my academic talking head.

and Somaesthetics seeks to re-attach the body to the academic head by exploring the legacy of Plato's body-soul antagonism. Shusterman draws on 20th-century philosophers like Michel Foucault, Ludwig Wittgenstein and especially Maurice Merleau-Ponty and John Dewey (Shusterman 2008). By using these scholars and studying the history of embodied practices we can acquire more diverse, choreo-linguistic metaphors (such as I propose with "impact") that better capture the connection between our minds, our bodies and the worlds around us. It may be that all philosophies are embodied philosophies, though a few are better positioned to understand the work of dancers.

In the academy, the fight to do what we are studying has been contentious. Clandinin and Connelly, key proponents of the essential Arts Practice method of research known as narrative inquiry, date the beginnings of their discipline to John Dewey's turn of the 19th- and 20th-century ideas on education (2004). Dewey sought to understand the student experientially, personally and socially. He stood against—and lost to—the normalized assembly-line methods proposed by Allan Bloom and widely adopted. Contemporary educators and artists like Emile Jaques-Dalcroze with his Eurythmics method of teaching music through movement followed on from the 19th-century "gymnastik" movement. Similar were the kinesthetic music of Robert Schumann and Françoise Delsarte's anachronistic understanding of the connection between the stage performer, their body and their emotions. During my undergraduate studies, I was certified in Dalcroze Eurythmics. This was a lifeline to me as classical music wrested sound from my body. The 20th century saw more methods emerge that Thomas Hanna might call "somatic" such as those of Bonnie Bainbridge Cohen, Moshé Feldenkrais and Frederick Matthias Alexander. During the early 20th-century, anthropologists Zora Neal Hurston and Katherine Dunham combined their practice as dancers, choreographers, writers and researchers. Despite these scholars' legacies and the potential of their methods for wider implementation, their ideas remain peripheral in the academy and are at best reduced to useful developmental techniques in music, dance and theatrical conservatories.

"The term 'Practice as Research' would probably not have been coined had artists not got involved with modern higher education institutions in respect of programs of learning, particularly at PhD level," (Nelson 2013: 3) Robin Nelson, an important author in the field, recounts. I will cite some New York City-based strands that have influenced my work. In the 1910s the Harlem Renaissance united innovative visual, textual and performance artists whose work and philosophy spread to institutions like Karamu House in Cleveland, where I had the privilege of performing twenty years ago. In the mid-20th century, the world of western visual art exploded in unprecedented ways, insidiously and delightfully infecting art schools and eventually universities. Artists like Yoko Ono, whose highly conceptual yet very practical works, "Cutting Piece" and "Bag Piece" (1964), brought artists together and challenged the intellectual foundations of art and performance in New York's Lower East Side (LES). My dance mentor, Maureen Fleming, formed part of this tradition in the early 1980s, helping to bring Japanese Butoh to America. She also developed a new minimalist dance aesthetic with the support of her mentor, theater pioneer and La Mama Experimental Theatre Club founder, Ellen Stewart. Between the postmodern developments of art schools and conservatories, the theoretical expansion of the humanities previously mentioned and the emergent field of Performance Studies (discussed in more detail later), foundations were laid in the 20th century for practice-based / practice-led / practice-as / Arts Practice research in the academy.

A couple of decades since the case for doctoral practice-as-research began, it has become all too easy to confuse terms. There are, however, important differences:

> Practice in practice-based research can be carried out freely for its own sake in order to produce artifacts. This is fairly similar to the general conception of art/design practice. On the contrary, practice in practice-led research is conscious

exploration with the knowledge involved in the making of artifacts. Second, the difference is in the roles of practitioner and researcher. In practice-based research, the practitioner's role may be more dominant than the researcher's role. The emphasis seems to be on practice, since a practitioner-researcher carries out her research solely based on her own practice. In practice-led research, the two roles appear to be equally important, because research becomes an intertwined part of practice. (Nimkulrat 2007: 2)

My own explorations of intimacy, violence and Irish step dance are practice-based insofar as my storytelling (scholastic writing) and my dancing (scholastic movement) both produce "artistic artifacts" that are created to stand alone. These outputs are of equal and independent value. These works could furthermore be described as practice-led in the sense that the writing and the dancing are of equal, "intertwined" value. Ultimately, the term used is not as important as the recognition of the various ways that readers of this project will approach the three major works: a thesis and two solo dance shows. I leave this distinction between practice-led versus practice-based and the assignment of academic and artistic authority up to the reader.

Moreover, I must acknowledge the role that academic theoretical discourse has played in this work. My scholarship stands in a close conversation with traditional Western methods of research in the arts and humanities (history and philosophy). In the making of both major dance works my choreography was formed in dialogue with my research according to two independent processes. This was a difficult approach for me to undertake. As Fiona Candlin observes, artists may worry that their academic work can take them too far away from their careers as artists, as evidenced by the fact that '[…]probably 90% of the formal discussions [she] had [with artists] were about the status and value of the written component' (Candlin 2000: 2). In the case of practice-as-research, academic research ought to be considered a practice in itself with its own attendant needs, power structures and opportunities for innovation. My efforts to engage with performance theory, Critical Race Studies, Critical Romani Studies and, if I may, Critical Irish Studies are complicated by the sentiment among sections of the academy that practice-as-research undermines the value of traditional PhDs and the field of dance research in general.

To explain how I tackle this problem, I shall return briefly to the American Irish Gaelic social experiment that I experienced during my upbringing in Cleveland. The seanchaí's stories were as educational as they were entertaining, and were performed alongside his wife's concertina music. This had the effect of allowing us to contemplate the lessons he taught on two different levels; on the level of oral text and on the level of music. David Hyde Pierce and so many involved in the formation of the *Conradh na Gaeilge,* or the Gaelic League, established a new standard for Irish social life in 1893 for many reasons, not the least being Irish independence from the British. While scholars have certainly exposed the complex gendered and racial boundaries with which Irish nationalism has been entwined including the much-studied North American context, there is a newer argument to be had—that Irish traditional cultural organizations are striving for a preservation of Irish indigeneity. This has certainly not been a singular, unifying project, but rather one that lays out a process of restoring and maintaining agency for Irish people in Irish culture. This community has taught me much and opened its doors to me, my dancing, my music and my storytelling research. I carry them all forward without placing any traditional art above another.

Irish indigeneity is something I do not seek to define as I was not born in Ireland, though I find value and truth in exploring what is "lost" within the Irish diasporic experience. In this connection, Arts Practice methodology helps me resolve the dilemma of doing versus writing. Helen Phelan at the University of Limerick Irish World Academy of Music and Dance began the Structured PhD program in Arts Practice in 2009. During my participation in this program I came to learn how our methodology places experts and their practices at the center of research in the arts. As someone trained in the traditional arts, I identify with this academic legacy and the program's emphasis on asserting what Susan Melrose would call the "expert intuition: of the artist within practice-as-research [PaR] in the arts" (Melrose 2006: 105). In my experience, the chief benefit of Arts Practice research is the expert artist-scholar's ability to tell and to show the value of what they do. Although no two Arts Practice researchers are alike, they all likewise occupy a liminal zone between the academic and the artistic worlds.

To return our discussion to an Irish Studies context, I cite Ó Dónaill's first definition of An Draoí: the druid. Na Draoiche (plural for Draoí) have historically been identified with the druids, ancient Irish priests famous for honoring trees in their religious practice. Druids could be considered shamans, poets or members of an artistic, learned and philosophical class. The history of druids, while fascinating, is highly contested and presents numerous challenges to academic research. In the Irish context, druids, indeed, can be thought of as artist-practitioners comparable to contemporary Arts Practice researchers. Though I do not consider myself to be standing in the forests of ancient Ireland in search of a Celtic Indigenous past, my choreography engages with the material forest surrounding me today. This objectual forest of trees-made-wooden clogs/ships/stocks is where the author, this contemporary Draoí stands. These haunted materials and their ghostly legacies linger in the world that I inhabit, they fill the air that I breathe and their roots connect me to my ancestry and to the ancestors of us all.

The Magician: Outlining Research Methodology

Dance research, particularly in early dance, prioritizes the study of dance via visual art, written accounts and dance manuals. This approach:

> [...] has resonances with the early study of butterflies, caught, killed and displayed upon a pin. This was, no doubt, of great benefit in the categorisation of butterflies, but ultimately produced a limited understanding of the butterfly as a living creature. In fact to say that the object presented on a pin is a butterfly presents a potentially dangerous barrier to understanding and enquiry, for it was a butterfly – it is now the corpse of a butterfly, which cannot be seen to exhibit the qualities and nature of 'butterfly' as living creature. No doubt certain attributes are 'inscribed' upon the corpse, but this fixity, while possibly helpful to a particular kind of reader, is a fundamental misrepresentation to those who wish to achieve a more complete understanding. (Bannerman 2006: 21)

The study of dance as a pinned butterfly via non-embodied methodology leads to problematic conclusions about historical subjects. Without rigorous critical analysis, this serves to reify whatever hegemonic biases the researcher carries with them. This can be seen in the case of E.A. Théleur's 1831 publication, *Letters on dancing, reducing this elegant and healthful exercise to easy scientific principles*, which goes to outlandish lengths to build a fictional, white supremacist history of dance. This book is considered to be one of the most important treatises on early Romantic ballet. It narrates the history of dance as follows:

> Dancing is made mention of as in use as far back as the ancient Egyptians; they gave festivals, where music and dancing pantomime made the principal features of the entertainments. This art was performed in most of their religious ceremonies and offerings to heathen deities.
>
> The Israelites, likewise, practised it at their ceremonies and offerings.

> To the Greek nation, particularly to the city of Athens, we are indebted, in early times, for great advancement of the art." (Théleur 1831: 2)

Théleur continues with an interpretation of dance in Ancient Greece and Rome. He goes on to suggest that the evolution of dance as an art form stopped after the fall of the Roman empire before making a sudden leap forward during the 15th century with the development of Italian court dance. Thereafter, dance was established at the court of the French King Louis XIV where it once again attained its classical grandeur. If we keep the butterfly of dance pinned to this page, the established narrative remains unchallenged. This narrative dictates that French ballet is the only true artistic dance form since it is rooted in Greco-Roman antiquity. Unfortunately, this claim remains largely unchallenged in early dance scholarship as I found to my surprise during a recent symposium on early dance at the University of Pennsylvania.[13]

On the other hand, if we unpin the butterfly; that is, if we critically consider and reconstruct the context of the author's work, other perspectives become possible. It is strange to consider that the seventeenth-century century Englishman Théleur, whose name was actually "Taylor", though he used a Gallic style in order to better his career as a dancing master, would be involved in the creation of any sort of dance connected with 2,000 year-old Eastern Mediterranean dance practices. Théleur merely recycles the Renaissance notion that the Greek muse Terpsichore fell asleep in ancient times only to awake in European imperial courts. We have little evidence of white European dance culture in the Middle Ages, though we know that dance was practiced continually by African, Romani, Middle Eastern, Asian and Native American peoples. Early dance researchers might consider that it is more likely that ballet was inspired by the dances of

---

13 The two-day Early Dance Symposium was titled "New Work on Old Dance: A Pre-1800 Dance Studies Symposium" and was hosted by the University of Pennsylvania February 22-24, 2024.

marginalized people living in Europe and by the cultures that European colonists were encountering. Perhaps it was only once the Church lost its authority during the Reformation and dancing was once again permitted that court dance developed on the basis of other world dance cultures. We find evidence of this in the popularity of morescas, canarios/canaries and other exotic, orientalist and blackfaced dance forms beginning in the second half of the 15th century, far earlier than typically supposed (Ndiaye 2022). These historical revisions are worth keeping in mind, particularly in the Romani case where during the late Middle Ages the Roma carried dance to Europe, subsequently playing a vital role in shaping European dance practices.

Moreover, the ancient sources used by early modern and even contemporary dance writers consist of sculpture, pottery, paintings and first-hand accounts. The study of early dance as a pinned butterfly serves to re-enact white supremacist fantasies of a whitened Ancient Greek (and African and Asian) ancestry. This privileging of a pinned (dead) approach to dance studies leads to the dismissal of living Black, Indigenous People of Color traditions as illegitimate art. What is more—in a true feat of mental acrobatics—many claim that these same committees stole their dances from the very colonizers who in fact stole it from them in the first instance. In the context of practice-based research, if we put the butterfly in motion, a new perspective emerges. Choreographers and dancers of court did not succeed in reviving Greek dance. However, their desire to do so reveals a lack of ancestral dance practices (or at least a reluctance to recognize them as such) and a desire to create a dance practice that sets them apart from and above the living dance traditions they would encounter or appropriate through colonialism.

I understand the process of studying something in motion as a form of *draíocht*, or magic. Catherine Foley describes, "[step] dancing is not fixed or fossilized. It is an embodied, dynamic, dance-music cultural activity that is constantly undergoing transformation according to transformations and interactions in, and between, step dancers, musicians, history, culture and society" (Foley 2013: 21). Foley, who has been foundational to the field of Irish traditional dance studies, uses an ethnochoreological approach to position Irish step dance within a hermeneutic arc that moves through the spaces of Irish step dance as taught by the Travelling Dancing Masters while bypassing British colonialism and the highly influential European continental style. The result is a rich, contoured and meaning-laden interpretation of Irish step dance history in its relationship with her own Kerry dance steps.

For dance scholars trained in schools of dead dance (dance that only lives in manuals, visual art and written accounts), the process of unpinning the butterfly appears as something magical: perhaps something miraculous but most likely an illusion or trick. For me, putting dance scholarship back in motion among those who have done the work of moving dance is magic of a healing sort. I recognize that as an Irish step dancer, the very steps and the tradition that I belong to extend back centuries to Irish traveling dance masters who adapted popular dances in the Atlantic world for an Irish context. I also identify with a long Romani tradition of dance which stands unbroken for thousands of years and which helped to usher in a new era of dance in Europe. The magic of unpinning the butterfly consists in realizing that I am part of something much greater than myself: an atemporal céilí with the ancestors.

For the wizard or magician (the third definition of An Draoí), practice requires methods of critical reflection and documentation for self and for posterity. For some there is the grimoire: the textbook of magic passed down through the generations. For many communities the ritual or dance is the method itself (Shea Murphy 2008):

> The ways many contemporary Native American dance pieces and practices directly challenged scholarly conceptions of valid history and historical markers (i.e. history documented through letters, decrees, facts, dates) likewise supported this understanding of dance's agency. Rather than only recounting history through dance, this choreographing and choreography

also present itself as historical research tool and document. In this way it suggested that contemporary Aboriginal stage dance functioned both as a way of researching an epistemological "way of knowing", with theoretical insight and historical legitimacy, and as itself embodied documentation, with archival value. (Shea Murphy 2008: 10)

In this thesis, I will elaborate on Foley's phenomenological understanding of Irish step dancing by exploring its Indigenous implications, explaining how tradition explodes our understanding of the present as exceptional or privileged. Chapter Five will more closely consider the construction of indigeneity and time in Irish step dance. The "magic" of Arts Practice research involves both approaches: a self-documenting multi-temporal dance practice and its documentation via writing (a grimoire). In other words, if I am to study Irish step dance I must actually do it. If I only observe Irish dance from a distance, I am only studying a 'corpse' of Irish dance. This can provide some knowledge, which I intend to share, but cannot truly penetrate into the process of Irish dancing. This is because in the act of creation, and also in the act of academic inquiry, there is "[…] a libidinal dimension or basis of knowledge activities—which is ignored or denied when we conceive of science and expertise as cognitive endeavors" (Knorr Cetina 2001: 195). When formulating an Irish dance, which can include re-representing traditional pre-set choreography, a "libidinal" quality is present. Such a lust for discovery was captured by Melrose's expert intuition. The yearning creative and inquisitive impulse is present in all parts of this doctoral research, and so it is essential that some system of documentation is in place to provide the fullest academic and artistic yield.

Defining Dance Research

As previously stated it is comparably easy to approach dance research as a clinical method of analyzing any patient culture. However, I argue that anthropological questions of agency also apply to a discipline's ability to "parasitically feed off" its subjects (Mercier 2016). I thus discourage a non-representative form of dance research and proclaim:

> '[…] the right of [Irish dance] to the ownership of [Irish dance] and to the unfettered control of [Irish dance] destinies, to be sovereign and indefeasible. The long usurpation of that right by a foreign people and government has not extinguished the right, nor can it ever be extinguished […]' (Clarke et al. 1916).

This re-wording of the Irish 1916 Proclamation to refer to Irish step dance might seem strange, if not offensive. However, if we define dance as a study of our own being and humanity, the objectification and ultimate dehumanization of dance becomes a problem of human rights. For example when we study Flamenco, are we studying a dance (a thing) or are we studying people who dance (an action)?[14] Dance has played a vital role in the perpetuation of stereotypes, such as the image of the savage Irish step dancer or the lascivious, exotic Romani "gypsy" dancer. If "[f]reedom is indivisible, and when one man is enslaved, all are not free" (Kennedy 1963), then the same could be said for the Irish dancer: when Irish dance is unable to assert its own rights and representation, it is enslaved under colonialism. My dance emerges from my academic research, and my academic research emerges from my dance. Irish dance is represented both in my research process and output. On a few occasions my supervisor has had to remind me to keep stepping, to keep my practice alive as I read and write. Nevertheless, this methodology represents an important step towards democratizing the field of research

---

14 "Flamencos" is what many Spanish Roma, Gitanos, Calé and Zincailli call each other and it represents a people as well as a culture. There is Romani-specific cartography inherent to this naming.

because the subject of study is given equal rights to the study itself. Furthermore, dance constitutes the object of the study, and as result impresses itself on my practice as a researcher.

When I refer to "Irish dance", I situate myself within a very large body of dance theory and history, employing a multi-artistic, multi-genre and research-driven approach to Irish dance. The question "What is Irish dance?" raises further historical, anthropological and commercial questions that, of course, evolve continually through practice. My approach is informed by historical and autoethnographic analysis. Today, the term "Irish dance" may refer to any dance that is practiced in Ireland or among Irish people. In the 19th century, the term was rarely used. Irish dance as name and practice was normalized, standardized and institutionalized in the 1890s, coinciding with the foundation of the Gaelic League. The work of the Gaelic League and that of later regulatory and funding bodies have drastically changed and continue to change the way Irish people in Ireland, America and elsewhere dance and think about "Irish" movement (Foley 2013). The process of "de-anglicizing Ireland"—still now underway—is built on understanding what it means to be Irish (Stewart 2000). At the Irish World Academy, the research potential of "Irish dance" moves in new directions and expands the academy by generating new knowledge and types of knowledge. This can include studies on de-colonization as well as broader questions of Irish-ness, indigeneity, place and identity. With regard to the present study, it allows me through dance to explore ideas of violent gesture, intimate touch and the human experience across time and space.

Arts-based researchers Mary Beth Cancienne and Celeste Snowber have argued that "[dance] is not only an expression of our research but a form of inquiry into the research process" (2003: 237). As a result, not only does reflecting on Irish dance and its history but also the very process of Irish dancing has the ability to uncover new knowledge. Dance researchers have gone a long way to showing that dance can "operate as a map connecting elements that could not otherwise be apprehended in isolation", echoing Smith and Fowle's observations on curation and helping us to understand these phenomena as a performance of male identity (Barrett and Bolt 2010: 12).

Irish dance as research is better understood in motion. Breandán de Gallaí's doctoral thesis, "*Imeall-Siúl*: a choreographic exploration of expressive possibilities in Irish step dancing," was the first academic work where scholarly text and Irish step dance choreography constituted both process and product (2013). In his thesis, de Gallaí draws on his experience as a prolific and high-profile Irish dancer and choreographer in non-profit and for-profit arts organizations to reflect on the form's neglected expressive capabilities. In my own dance research, I draw on Irish dance's ability to construct time and place, thereby asserting the need to understand Irish-ness in motion. This approach connects identity to practice, drawing history, tradition and theory into its murky depths.

A First Person, a Second and a Third: Building responsible reflexes in practice

Written documentation in Arts Practice research is at least partly intended to quell institutional "anxiety" surrounding "the apparent difficulty of judging the intellectual and scholarly worth of artwork" (Candlin 2000). If the process of creating work is documented and converted into a thesis, the demands of doctoral research are met and the insecurities of the university are abated. In a sense, we are still subjugating things to our study of them. Some researchers, however, cite more positive reasons for the process of documentation: "to make the creative process somewhat transparent by capturing each step the practitioner-researcher takes in the process, both consciously and unconsciously" (Nimkulrat 2007: 4). This debate is relevant to my research, though I am required to document my PhD research process. This is a Transatlantic phenomenon: I am part of an academic institution and therefore must submit. As long as this remains true, it is impossible to tell if creative researchers truly do wish to engage in forms of written documentation, or if they affectionately turn to it out of a kind of Stockholm syndrome. Fortunately this is not where the matter rests.

Something interesting happens when the methods of narrative inquiry and autoethnography come up against the bulwark of academia. Narrative inquiry and autoethnography do not depose the academic puppeteer, nor force him to the stage or to the page. Rather, they recognize him as part of the performance of research and a part of the dance encounter. Documentation need not only be a process of demonstrating academic rigor and process. It can also be a means of gaining representation for myself through all stages of research.

The assertion of the right of individuals to represent themselves in government and academia stand in contradiction to the rhetoric of capitalism and colonialism. Peter Linebaugh and Marcus Rediker, authors of *The Many-Headed Hydra: Sailors, Slaves, Commoners, and the Hidden History of the Revolutionary*

Atlantic, re-interpret the history of early modern colonialism, arguing that:

> [...] peoples of the world have, throughout history, clung stubbornly to the economic independence that comes from possessing their own means of subsistence, whether land or other property, European capitalists had to forcibly expropriate masses of them from their ancestral homelands so that their labor-power could be redeployed in new economic projects in new geographic settings. This dispossession and relocation of peoples have been a worldwide process spanning five hundred years. (Linebaugh and Rediker: 2013: 17)

Linebaugh and Rediker's understanding of the economics, politics, and theology of the early modern world emphasize the urge on the part of the upper classes to privatize the "commons" and to sell it back to the people from whom it was taken. They offer a profound re-interpretation of the term "grand larceny". For Linebaugh and Rediker, furthermore, there can be little doubt that the philosophers of the early modern age—John Dee, René Descartes, John Locke, et al.—contributed to developing the apparatus of colonialism. The academy is thus indicted on the charge of conspiracy to advance economic imperatives that run contrary to the public interest.

Stephen Quaye has observed that, "Many people in academe have built their prestigious careers and statuses based on the lives of people in far less privileged positions; this is highly problematic" (2007: 4). Indeed, academia continues to exemplify commercial, expropriative values. These values are hegemonic and markedly different from those of marginalized people. The academy prefers one truth and the marginalized many truths, stories or personal perspectives. Some autoethnographers would propose that the answer to this problem is not to dismantle academia, but to challenge who is allowed into the academy and to re-evaluate what research methods are valid. When the researched are allowed to research themselves and to involve their own ethics in the research process, not only is the exploitative nature of the process somewhat redressed, but the quality of the research is also improved. Furthermore, when we recognize the existence of different social values, such as the differences between dance carried out in familial/community contexts and dance carried out for profit, fame or career advancement, our knowledge is improved.

Narrative inquiry offers a further qualitative approach to social science and humanities research. For the inventors of this concept, Jean Clandinin and Michael Connelly, narrative inquiry presents "[…] the best way of representing and understanding experience" (2004: 18). Narrative inquiry is based on the idea that "[narrative] is both the phenomenon and the method of the social sciences" (Ibid.). To conduct their research, narrative inquirers must "[…] make themselves as aware as possible of the many, layered narratives at work in their inquiry space" (Clandinin and Connelly: 18,70). This extends from Lyotardian "grand narratives" to the narratives of the research to the personal narratives of the researcher (Lyotard 1984). The process of recognizing the layered nature of the inquiry and refining one's storytelling is essential for grappling with violence and its legacies in Irish step dance. By applying a lens of narrative inquiry, we discover that all forms of early dance research tell a story regardless of whether or not they claim to be objective. Moreover, in this way, all research comes to be seen as practice-based. The difference between traditional academic research and practice-based research in the strict sense is that the latter strives to reckon its own narratives in the process of doing the work.

The Irish dance pieces that I created for this project draw on the work of narrative inquirers and Indigenous autoethnographers. Paul Whitinui writes that "Indigenous autoethnography as a distinct 'Native' method of inquiry requires that as a person of Māori descent, I respectfully introduce 'who I am' (social identity) and 'where I am from' (place identity)" (2013: 458). Whitinui contextualizes the Māori and their narrative techniques within the research narratives that study them. This unveils not only new information, but also the potential of research to "replenish" people, their community and their environment (2013: 480). I employ Indigenous autoethnographic practices in order to grasp the native and colonial narrative practices present in my work (discussed further in the next chapter). Through these techniques, all voices—first person, second and third—gain representation.

The last method of documentation I wish to mention consists of video recording and visual mind-mapping. My laptop computer, tablet and mobile phone have allowed me to document non-text "epistemic artifacts" that I have encountered during my research (de Gallaí 2013). These artifacts, along with text-based journal entries, were entered in and/or linked to entries in Evernote, a multi-platform app that allows the user to easily date and organize entries. During my research process I also used mind-maps, which spatially visualize text and image information with lines representing connections. I will not be sharing any of these artifacts in the present dissertation as they were simply part of the process of developing the three major works I submit for this doctorate. My journal entries, mind-maps and video recordings capture earlier versions of what you are reading (and seeing) here, and will continue to evolve with my practice past the submission of this dissertation.

In total, my methods of academic research strive to create an "expert/creative meta-practice" which is informed by my training in academia and as an Irish dance artist (Melrose 2007), as well as being personally supported by my inherited and trained traditions. The end goal is simple, to create Arts Practice research "[...] as a form of language, [where] art can become reflexive, turn on itself, invite us to question our own premises, to ask, how do I see? What can I know? How do I know what I know? Then, art becomes a process and form of inquiry" (Bochner and Ellis 2003: 508).

The Augur: Theoretical Frameworks/ Underpinnings

The last definition of An Draoí I wish to cite is the augur, the one who interprets natural signs in the hope of foretelling the future. Since my theoretical framework rests on objects and our relationships to them, references to divination, superstition and mystery offer helpful points of departure. My understanding of performance, the body and practice supports this process. I explain my use of them in the following.

My Introduction to Performance Studies

At the end of my first semester in my master's degree at NYU Glucksman Ireland House, my faculty advisor suggested that I take a course in the Performance Studies Department. Having been confident that I knew what Performance Studies was, I came to discover that it is not so easy to define. The course descriptions made little sense to me and the philosophical references none. I was offended that André Lepecki thought I was not suited for his "seminar on dance theory: dance and the political." He said the only class I could handle was a course on social dance.

I wore a suit jacket and tie to my first day of class, so to the other students I looked like I was ready to sell car insurance. The room was full of various types of New York artists, including ones who appropriated Romani and Palestinian fashions and accused me of dressing too homonormative (in other words I was not enough of a countercultural gay). Pretense aside, the promise of Performance Studies to me was clear: any process or identity was up for debate, discussion and research, provided you have the fluency in Performance Studies jargon. Among the student population of the department I found a circle of international and diverse people acquires more international and diverse knowledge, particularly with regard to the mediation of difference.

The lectures, performances and conversations I took part in during that semester revolutionized my understanding of performance, human interaction and my own Irish-American identity. I learned that Performance Studies is about developing a research voice capable of critically observing the hegemonic, oppressive and appropriative while supporting the agency of the subaltern, sonic, natural, Black, Indigenous, Queer and Feminine. It was also about discovering a deeper yet paradoxically more obvious understanding of the way the world works: the way the world performs. My research into Irish dance was shattered. Throughout the semester my orientation as a researcher was reshaped in ways that exposed the white-washed histories of dance I had grown up with. The suppressed historical legacies of the Black Atlantic (Gilroy 1993) and maritime dance (Brown 2022) changed my understanding of my own whiteness. At the same time, I came to grasp the shifting meanings of sound in dance history and the way that Irish-ness responds to colonialism and globalization.

The paper I submitted that semester would form the beginning of the present research. I have kept in touch with a few classmates and two professors from the course on social dance, while other students clearly demonstrated I was not worthy to move in their circles. In hindsight this is curious to me as if I had made them aware of my involvement in the Royal Iconic House of LaBeija (a well-known community of Vogue dancers), I would have been seen as part of the in-crowd. But I was in poverty at that time, living on disability benefits and serving my own Ballroom/House "realness": I was trying to pass for one of the wealthy, white and sophisticated graduate students I saw all over campus. I felt, perhaps wrongly, that these budding academics did not actually care about the survival and success of New York's QTBIPOC communities; that they did not understand Ballroom/House, pier life and Vogue; and that they could not fathom the realities of sex work, HIV/AIDS, EBT cards,[15] racism and transphobic-motivated murder that stalked the community but did not define life within it. In any case, my time studying in the department was over and it was time to return to Glucksman Ireland House (GIH) and to finish my master's degree. I never received an invitation to return to the Performance Studies Department, or to Lepecki's course. Later I came to understand how important this department was and how famous some of its members are, though I had no idea at the time. My supervisor at GIH hoped that I would get to know and perhaps received mentorship from his friend, the queer scholar José Estaban Muñoz. Sadly he had died prior to the beginning of my studies in December 2013. This is part of a much larger, older story of intergenerational loss in queer and trans communities through oppression, marginalization and criminality. I would have to find my own way and define performance on my own terms.

---

15 New York State's public assistance card.

Defining Performance, Practice and the Body

Performance Studies emerged in the wake of Victor Turner's project of attempting to make the field of anthropology more critical of its methodologies; the birth of the University of Paris VIII in the wake of uprisings in 1968 and the first "happenings" in New York City. According to Lakoff and Johnson's *Metaphors to Live By*, the bodily senses—seeing, smelling, sensing, awakening, etc.—have long been used as linguistic metaphors (2003). For new age spiritualists, for example, to awaken from sleep is to know via "awakening". For Richard Schechner, similarly, performing is a form of knowing. Schechner's understanding of performance acquired a new meaning as a linguistic metaphor: "The acceptance of the performative as a category of theory as well as a fact of behavior has made it increasingly difficult to sustain the distinction between appearances and facts, surfaces and depths, illusions and substances." (Schechner 1998: 362) The instability of the act of performing and our definition of it continues to complicate our understanding of performativity. Performance was and in many cases still is a specialist pursuit. The notion of performativity implies that there is some sort of audience that is doing the spectating. In my experience in the field and according to Susan Melrose, the Performance Studies researcher is typically the one doing the watching. Performance studies can thus be understood as a form of "spectator studies", or business as usual in academia:

> What is designated then, by Performance Studies uses of the term 'the body', is a theatricalized site (as well as sight); what it articulates can be 'mapped', from the peculiar position of spectating, with all of the ideologically-specific implications of the cartographer's position of power and overview. (Melrose 2006: 100)

This is an old debate, and one I cite here in order to situate this project. While I think Melrose's observation is valid, I nevertheless find Performance Studies methods to be a necessary counterpart to practice. Labeling Performance Studies as spectator studies is an oversimplification of the matter as no academic discipline can develop without being responsive to the economic and institutional factors that gave rise to them or the privileges of its members. Richard Schechner's "[…] 'broad spectrum' approach addresses […] the need for performing arts departments to recuperate what rightly belongs to them" (Schechner 1989). In the mid-20th century, theatre and dance departments had abandoned the intellectual aspects of studying performance to pursue the work of preparing performers for work in dance or theatre. Schechner, a theatre practitioner himself, sought to restore control of the discipline to those who know it best, namely the performers. The metaphor of human and even non-human behavior as performance became useful for empowering dancers, musicians, actors to join in academic discourse, thereby profoundly transforming the fields of philosophy, art and design. When developing his program of Performance Studies, Schechner re-"distributed the sensible" (Rancierre 2006), taking a verb associated exclusively with doing and applying it to the process of knowing. His ideas had significant consequences for artistic developments in both academia and society at large.

A related but different metaphor has come about through the word "practice." When theorists such as Susan Melrose, Christopher Bannerman or Karin Knorr Cetina use the word practice—something that is usually quite banal but essential to a performer— they re-purpose it in a similar manner to Schechner's repurposing of "performance". Both words are similar insofar that both practice and performance require repetition; if it is not "twice-behaved", it is not a performance (Schechner 1998: 361); nor, indeed, is it practice. The difference is that practices are generally characterized by a greater number of events, perhaps amounting to over 10,000 hours (Colvin 2010). This opens the door to conversations on the nature of expertise, and whether all practices are in fact epistemic. As mentioned previously, Arts Practice research is concerned with studying expert intuition. This distinguishes it from Performance Studies which tends to view all performance as being of equal theoretical interest.

Before I contextualize this argument within my research, I must further explain "the body" and theories of embodiment and somatics. Sean Gallagher's research on the body uses the language of cartography "[as] an attempt to redefine the terrain, to redraw, or perhaps to erase the boundaries between body and mind, the vocabulary of embodiment is thus intended to serve as an integrative remapping [...]" of phenomenological, scientific, cognitive, expression and environmental components (Gallagher 2006: 244). In this manner, the act of Irish dancing in the context of Arts Practice research can be understood as an "integrative remapping" of Irish-ness, as well as other identities and concepts with which I or other Irish step dancers associate. In my own research I avoid the "severe mapping" endemic to traditional academic research (MacDonald 2016), and instead focus on the way in which the dancing body travels in time and thereby re-writes our understanding of it.

In the Irish context, it is impossible to escape a "somatic" approach to the body in dance. The choreographic approaches of Bonnie Bainbridge Cohen (Body-Mind Centering), Rosemary Butcher and Anna Halprin have been central to the Irish contemporary dance scene since the 1990s and 2000s, so much so that at the Irish World Academy contemporary dance is synonymous with somatic dance. Within the Arts Practice program we were required to undertake a week of immersion in somatic dance practice and documentation. I was familiar with these practices since they had formed part of American public education in the '80s and '90s. However, I was unaware of the history of the Judson Dance Movement despite having actually attended services at a Judson Memorial Church on many occasions.16 I found that somatic practitioners tend to over-emphasize the independence of the body from its environment (or indeed the mind). As a result somatic dance can risk privileging body over mind and environment. This is especially the case

---

16 I live on Gay Street, a five-minute walk from Judson Church in the Greenwich Village of New York City.

where the bodies in question have access to clean, empty dance studios where one can take one's shoes off without it connoting poverty. In the viral social media assignment, "What's classy if you're rich but trashy if you're poor?", barefoot dance could be named alongside bilingualism and consanguineous marriage (Davis 2020). Ultimately, I found Irish contemporary dance in contrast to "form"-based dance to be liberating. I felt a sense of freedom in somatic practice, particularly when dancing with my friends and local dance community in North Clare (discussed in Chapter Five). This also enabled me to recognize the conflict that exists between Irish contemporary dance and Irish step dance. This conflict reflects wider debates between tradition and contemporaneity, form and feeling. The many choreographic differences between the two forms are not new but in fact form part of how these dance forms came to be and continue to evolve. When creating my first major work, *The Querist*, I found somatics particularly useful. In my second work, *AngelAI*, a somatic approach to Irish step dance (or an Irish step dance approach to somatic practice) was the way forward.

The ruling cognitive metaphor for my study must be one that understands its own responsiveness to and affect evolving media and technology. I draw inspiration from Andrew Pickering, who made an important discovery concerning the relationship between scientific history and theory when he wrote of, "exploring some directions in which analyses of scientific practice at the microlevel can be suggestively extended to macrosocial concerns." (Pickering 2001: 172) Pickering discusses how organic chemistry evolved as a result of the needs of the dye industry, how the experience of shock and panoramic seeing emerged because of trains and Marxism emerged entirely because of the industrial revolution. In a similar vein, I argue that ideas of performance, practice and the body emerge because of the changing world we live in. Our theories of behavior go awry when we view these as independent phenomena. A cautious respect for this relationship between economies of cash and economies of ideas forms the basis of my definitions of HTE, psychometric theory, intimate violence and impact-driven dance.

An increasingly popular word within Arts Practice research that is likely to increase its popularity is curation. The idea of curation has become especially relevant in the age of the internet, which contains an unprecedented volume of information that must be organized, or "curated" by consumers and web developers. Following Pickering's methodology, we can see that curation as a practice and curatorial thinking (both conscious and unconscious) are emerging from vast worlds of communication and connection that surround us. Therefore the act of curation can be understood as a form of a practice or performance. However, the word "curation" has a nuance that performance and practice do not possess, suggesting the ability of the curator to conduct theoretical and administrative work (as fraught as these may be) and to do so as practice. In this way, the notion of "curation" eliminates the problem of whether performers or practitioners are "thinking" performers and practitioners. It also grants some agency to all of us who must curate deluges of information on a daily basis. On my journey to understand object relationships in Irish step dance, the framework of curation opened doors to complex, conflicting and less positive relationships and discoveries. It has allowed Irish contemporary dance practices and Irish traditional step dance to stand the two pillars of my practice, separate but supporting the whole of the dance.

An Draoí as augur or diviner is someone with psychic ability who can interpret natural phenomena, especially the movement of birds, or read oracles (such as cards, water dowsing or crystals) to predict the future. As performance, practice or curation theorists, we are constantly reading our surroundings to better understand where we have been and where we are now. Sometimes we also use our prophetic gaze to better understand where we are going. When we enter the domain of the somatic however, intuition in all its power must be acknowledged alongside the phenomena that our philosophical minds interpret. In the context of my own work, this is the work of The Psychometrist.

Summary

This chapter has explained what should not be taken for granted in research: who we are, how our identity informs what we do, how our research can be situated within the academy and what ideas and terminology predicate inquiry. At risk of tautology, in this chapter and throughout this project I will be arguing for the value of first-person narratives and lived experiences in research, be they historical, practical or theoretical in nature. It is risky, difficult work but also in many ways easier to carry out when we no longer allow our identities as "academic researchers" to limit what we are researching. In the case of historical research, are we allowing presuppositions about our sources to limit the questions we are willing to ask of history? In the case of impact-driven dance, are we prepared to question white nationalists who have spread narratives about past tradition that erase from the dance those who most acutely felt the impact of colonialism?

The chapter began with recounting some key events in my life, going from the joy of dancing in a traditional community to the loneliness of solo performance within modern dance spaces. I discussed isolation as a form of trauma and explained my trauma-led approach to the history of early modern dance and technology. My identities as an Irish traditional step dancer and dance historian led me to Ireland to begin my Arts Practice research. This process led me to acknowledge the privileges and power imbalances that exist within the academy, who has typically been allowed to participate and who has not.

In the next section I discuss my methodology, which combines autoethnography, mind-mapping and dance as documentation and product. Using my dual methodology as a historian—or, if I may, a storyteller—and dancer, I present this thesis as being of independent and equal value to the creative works it accompanies. Thus, in my chapters on my two dance works I will not be striving to explain them or their creation in any strict or clear way, but will rather focus on my personal discovery of violence in dance.

Finally, this chapter defined what I mean when I write of the body, embodiment, performance, practice and curation. As this research uses post-human performativity to help me discover the phenomena of impact-driven dance, I have found the cognitive linguistics of curation to be most helpful. This will become clear in the following chapter as we move to explore how dance and our identification with it can function curatorially through encounter.

Chapter Three:

The Psychometrist

[Left foot in front]
Jump, kick, hop back-234
Jump, kick, hop back-234
Jump, kick, hop back-234
Hop, hop back, hop back-234

This chapter lays out a lived, theoretical framework for a multi-temporal, choreographic study of objects. The study of the role of objects in our lives and the way we identify cuts across a variety of processes, theories and academic disciplines. In this project I propose a psychometric theory for dance research which will enable a better understanding of the encounter between an impact-driven dancer and the materials and phenomena of their practice. Psychometry, I argue, can be understood as a kind of soul-reading of objects. My choreographic practice is informed by the disciplines that have shaped my dance: Feminism, Queer and Trans Studies, Disability Studies and Critical Romani Studies.

 The previous chapter situated my identity within American and Irish academic and dance spaces, explaining how my experiences of dance have shaped the knowledge and methods of this research. Building on an autoethnographic Arts Practice methodology, my practice as an Irish traditional step dancer and historian of dance and technology has evolved from my lived experience and been informed by the communities that have helped me to understand my "discoveries". I seek to guard the agency of the communities from whom I have learned these methods of knowing and to thwart the colonial, academic tendency to claim discovery of that which has already been discovered by someone else. I do, at the same time, lay claim to a lived experience moving within these communities. I hope in this way to encourage others to step through their own complex, conflicting layers of identifications.

During my master's research, Performance Studies introduced me to Queer academic perspectives. My study in Queer theory helped me understand how the meaning of an object can be reshaped by a marginalized community—often subverting the original purpose of the object. In what follows, I recount my experience as a young adult, gay Irish step dancer. Next, I introduce the notion of psychometric practice drawing on new materialism, post-humanism and the concept of the somatechnic. This framework is grounded in feminism and Trans Studies, which is fitting as the majority of my mentors and friends have been cisgender and transgender women. Their knowledge, wisdom and guidance have enveloped and nurtured my life as an effeminate cisgender male. The practices and insight they have shared with me may be beyond my full understanding, but this does not preclude me from citing and acknowledging them. Through their insights, I have become aware of many facets of my own identity which have guided my understanding of Irish step dance.

At the same time as I sought to develop a Queer Feminism of Irish step dance, I also drew on a practical dance and Disability Studies perspective. Disability Studies came to my attention by chance in 2016 when I was working with performers in Galway living with intellectual disability. I myself live with three disabilities and for almost a decade of my life relied on the support of New York City's disability assistance programs. As such, working with and learning from these artists was greatly informative. Through their work I came to learn how my own disabilities have shaped my dance and embodied connection to the world. For example, my hearing disability has reduced the auditory dimension of step dance and enhanced the somatic. Moreover, my 2013 diagnosis of post-traumatic stress disorder completely reshaped my relationship to traumatic histories. My subsequent treatment helped to understand how dancing with traumatic histories and their artifacts can serve as a kind of exposure therapy.[17]

The last major facet of my identity that has informed my understanding of the relationship of objects and intimate violence and impact is that of my Romani identity. During my academic journey I have come to a better understanding of Black dance and the suppression of Blackness via white supremacy, colonialism and racism. When I refer to Blackness I mean the experiences of people of color. In my family this included those with black and brown skin tones who have suffered from the impact of anti-Romani racism. In Ireland and Europe my experience of gypsyism and anti-Romani racism spurred me to stop hiding behind my white-passing identity and embrace, critically engage with and feel my Romani identity. This complex and often painful journey unveiled much within the dance, and helped me to face and embrace the legacy of my Romani inheritance. Some of this I share here as it relates to impact-driven dance, and has allowed me to draw my conclusions about the Blackness of Irish step dance (more on this in Chapter Five).

I summarize these autoethnographic human–technological encounters through the medium of psychometry, or object soul-reading. A psychometric approach, I believe, allows for greater agency of feeling, knowing and asking in spaces where previously academic interpretation and translation have dominated. This is

---

17 Dance contains many elements of exposure therapy: a recreation of the violence, a re-exposure to the objects related to violence, the crafting of an embodied story that can then be re-experienced on a regular basis, thus reducing the disruptive impact of the original traumatic event while helping the traumatized individual to re-contextualize the trauma within in their lives. The transformation of trauma into an artistic, restorative and generative practice that produces agency for the dancer is a goal of my own dance work and of this project.

helpful in dance scholarship as well as practice since lesser agency is given to historiographic, literary or political interpretations of impact-driven dance, while the problematic task of feeling the dance is re-asserted. The intimate encounter of objects can be political, metaphorical or historical, though it should not be understood exclusively through this lens. As I have learned from my exploration of identities marginalized within myself, the moment of impact with objects is a moment—if we so choose—of pain and suffering that nevertheless points the way to heart, body and soul. The theory of psychometric dance implies that we constantly experience the world as it is and how we want it to be in our very own bodies and lays direct claim to that experience, particularly in cases where that encounter or a history of that kind of encounter has been unacknowledged or denied.

Reverse Psychometry

The medium spoke to the air and drew
A wooden clog. In Lily Dale the dead
Do not die while the living learn death's dance.
Generations of seers sat with me
As the water rose in crayon around
The floating shoe—a message meant for me.

Psychometrists read objects but today,
The Spirit World showed the object read me.

Paraphrase

My life has been steeped in practices of intuition that were encouraged and nurtured by both my mother and father's family. These practices included not just dance but various forms of divination, prophecy, cartomancy and mediumship with the Spirit world and worlds beyond, though we never used such names. Each of these practices are rich topics for academic investigation. However, this would take us beyond the scope of our inquiry. Nevertheless, I would like to appropriate a term from this spiritual milieu called "psychometry", or the ability to know facts about an object by merely touching it.

My family did not commonly practice psychometry, although it would not have raised suspicion if any of us, upon touching an object, acquired a special sense of it or its carrier. I came to practice psychometry with greater rigor (tested blindfolded with random objects) when I joined the Spiritualist movement in 2010. I studied it closely at the Arthur Findlay College in Stansted, England during the first few years of my doctoral studies while I was living in Ireland.18 During this time I witnessed a resurgence in Spiritualism in Ireland in all its forms which overlapped with more native spiritual practices. Spiritualism in Ireland has a long history that includes such figures as W.B. Yeats, who was greatly interested in the occult, particularly as it was informed by Irish mythology and folklore. Suffice it to say for now that Spiritualism, the parapsychological and the paranormal is not entirely out-of-place in Irish culture in general or Irish step dance in particular.

While the role of spiritual practice, religion and the occult in Irish society and culture is not the subject of this study, I find a mystical framework to be helpful. Mysticism both commands respect and garners suspicion for the still yet unknown, which includes the worlds of meaning, use, and purpose hidden in the objects in our everyday life. In the stanzas that opened this section I recount an inexplicable, mysterious event that took place in the summer of 2021 at the Spiritualist camp of Lily Dale, New York when a third generation Spirit-artist/medium drew a wooden clog at the beginning of my reading with her. Given the significance of wooden shoes in my research and the many serendipitous experiences I have had with clogs, this was uncanny. She could not have known neither me nor my research, since none of my work was published or publicly accessible at the time. That year I was in the process of finishing a piece about wooden shoes, wooden ships and maritime dance. As striking as this coincidence is, I leave aside the question of belief in order to allow for curiosity, caution and An Draoí. As I continue to move through identities, I will apply to each one the core concepts of psychometry: the reading of objects, touch-knowing (embodied encounter) and the potential for things to know us better than we know them.

---

18 According to the National Spiritualist Association of Churches, "Spiritualism is the Science, Philosophy, and Religion of continuous life, based upon the demonstrated fact of communication, by means of mediumship, with those who live in the Spirit World" ("National Spiritualist Association of Churches," n.d.).

The Gay: Queer, Trans, Feminist Somatechnics

Time travel to the set of an Irish television show in Las Vegas, Nevada. We were five Irish step dancers led by the dance teacher, adjudicator, choreographer and original *Riverdance*-r Ronan McCormack.[19] Producer Anne Stirling had conceived of a television series comprising six episodes, each of which explored a different part of the contemporary Irish dance world. Commissioned by RTÉ and BBC Northern Ireland, *Jigs and Wigs* was shot in the summer of 2013 by Stirling Productions (Jigs & Wigs - Viva Las Vegas! 2014), a Belfast-based television company that had produced other programs featuring Irish step dance. Each episode of *Jigs and Wigs* considered the "more unusual members of the Irish dance world". The purpose of ours was to probe the male experience. Given the high ratio of women to men in Irish dance, the male experience could be considered unusual. The "wrinkle" in this time and space was that the producers were secretly exploring the *gay* male experience (L'Engle 2007).[20]

For this episode, Ronan picked male dancers he knew directly or by word-of-mouth to be homosexual. The six of us formed the group "Men in Kilts". The fact that we were gay, however, was never made explicit on the TV program. Only one member agreed to be out about his sexuality, while the rest of us preferred our privacy.[21] We were filmed reality-tv style during four days of rehearsal in a studio outside the Vegas strip as well as while we were marching and dancing in the Las Vegas Pride Parade and during our three-minute performance at the Pride Festival. Until

---

19 Ronan danced in the original Eurovision production of Riverdance, as well as subsequent productions. He is a well-respected TCRG and ADCRG within the *An Comisiúin le Rincí Galeacha*. He adjudicated my dancing at the 2008 Mid-Atlantic Oireachtas.

20 I use the term "gay" as this is prior to my own awareness of the academic "queer" label. Gay is the former term used to describe the predominately white-male homosexual experience in an Irish drama context (O'Brien 2014).

21 Since this time all of us have been out about our sexuality online and in social media;

the air date, we had no idea what would air of the large quantity of footage taken of us.

A decade later this program seems very reasonable, even desirable in a post-Marriage Equality Referendum Ireland.[22] At the time of the shoot however, my previous experiences in showbusiness and in the Irish dance world in Los Angeles, New York City and Dublin had seriously hindered my ability to perform the role of the out-and-proud gay man. It is often uncertain how homophobia affects its victims or indeed whether or not it is happening. Working in showbiz meant being open to homophobia. This eroded my confidence and, ultimately, well-being and health. When I was on set for *Jigs & Wigs* I had invented a story about my sexuality crafted after a decade of difficult encounters with teachers, managers, agents, industry experts, family and friends telling me to "shut up" about my sexuality; I lied. I said I was not gay, but "open" to either gender.

The episode premiered in February 2014 with the following caption:

> 'Jigs and Wigs' features some of the more unusual individuals and their stories which make Irish dancing a vibrant and progressive entertainment phenomenon. Episode 4 Viva Las Vegas – feising in Las Vegas. In a world where everything is make believe, male Irish dancers live their own fairy-tale in a pageant to rival anything else seen on the Vegas Strip during Gay Pride Week. (Jigs and Wigs 2017)

Our gayness was shaded and hidden in a spectacle of secrecy. Ireland's National Television and Radio Broadcaster managed to present three strands of my life that I had begun exploring in New York's downtown theater and performance art world: Irish dance, fairy-tales and homosexuality. While I often spoke about my sexuality, sometimes even on stage, I hid many of the struggles I had experienced with my same-sex attraction, my queer life

---

22 The 2015 Marriage Equality Referendum of Ireland was a public vote that legalized same-sex marriages. Two weeks later the United States Supreme Court made the *Obergefell* ruling which did the same.

and otherworldly attractions within the myths and fairy-tales that supported my Irish traditional dance works. Ironically, I had even aspired to produce Vegas-style Irish traditional dance entertainment which would transport other Irish-Americans to a mythic Ireland, one romantically lost in time that could help us explore our confused (or in the case of first or second generation Irish, soon-to-be confused) identity and connection to Ireland. I did not, at any time, wish to apply a label to my queerness or to use it as a vehicle for self-promotion. Being gay has always been a mysterious thing to me, and my sense of myself as an artist has always made most sense to me understood within the realm of the mystic.23 As I danced with this project, psychometry would help me to honor a fantastical instrument that has helped me to navigate what has been at times violent homophobia.24

As I look back, the summer of 2013 brought another twist of fate that guided the evolution of my dance and this PhD. During my nearly two decades in New York I could seldom afford adequate studio space for the dancing I needed to practice every day, so I rehearsed my jigs, reels and hornpipes on the wooden planks of the piers of New York City. While preparing an audition for a new *Cirque du Soleil* show on the Christopher Street Pier (a job I did not get), Celso Satori LaBeija and Jamil LaBeija of the Royal House of LaBeija approached me and told me they were Vogue dancers. I had been dancing the traditional set dance, "The King of the Fairies" with moves inspired by an Australian pole dancer I was dating at the time. I knew very little of this artform, but I was drawn to their moves. Over that summer I continued to meet Celso and Jamil at the pier, in Washington Square Park and

---

23 Although I had helped host, as a cocktail waiter, at Therapy Lounge in NYC the first two official screenings of RuPaul's Drag Race on Logo Network, I could not believe that there would ever, anywhere be a significant or financially sustaining demand for queer art, and certainly not in a space of "gay" and "Irish dance".

24 I should also mention that while I am a cisgender male, I have not always been interpreted as one or dressed to cisgender male standards. I have experienced physical violence as a result of this.

in the club. On the water, on subway platforms waiting for trains, in gym studios and in my tiny studio, I began to Step *and* Vogue.

I will go into further choreographic detail in the next chapter about how Step&Vogue evolved alongside my research, culminating in a theatrical dance work that featured dance happenings around Ireland in clubs, train platforms, theaters and gym studios. For now, as I revisit the Irish Otherworld (the domain of the fairy or the *sídhe*) and Irish step dance in a queer context, I will introduce the Queer and Feminist theory that supported my critical engagement with Step&Vogue helped me to translate embodied knowledge into academic knowledge.

Subculture, the Meaning of Style by Dick Hebdige begins with a discussion of Jean Genet's arrest by the Spanish Police, which involved the confiscation of a tube of Vaseline (1979). This ordinary household item assumed a different meaning in the eyes of the Spanish police; it was evidence of crimes of homosexuality. For Genet, this object carried enormous significance, representing "triumph" even in the face of scorn and ridicule in the police station. For Hebdige, the horrific violation of a queer man's privacy via law enforcement's moral objections to synthetic grease shows how "[the] meaning of subculture is… always in dispute, and style is the area in which the opposing definitions clash with most dramatic force." (Ibid.: 3) The idea that an object carries a particular, special meaning in subcultural or marginal contexts profoundly altered how I perceived my relationships to the materials of Irish step dance: the ghillie soft shoes typically meant for women and children, the seldom-worn-nowadays kilt, as well as the performance of gendered foot gestures; indeed, the artform itself. Perhaps for Queer and Trans Irish step dancers, each of these objects carries a different or additional meaning than it does for cis and heterosexual dancers. I began dancing toe stands[25] in show choreography in 2006, a decade before it was

---

25 To perform a "toe stand" is to stand on the toe tip of the Irish dance hard shoe, similar to dancing *en pointe* in ballet. Turns, taps and even jumps are performed while dancing in toe stands.

adopted by male Irish step dancers. At the time, toe stands in hard shoes as well as rocks and brushes were taboo for men[26] and my use of them was frowned on in the highly regulated competitive dance sphere. For me, however, it was an expression of my identity. Furthermore, it required expert, rigorous engagement and practice to carry forth that personal meaning. I could not simply dance the kinds of toe stands that I saw the girls and women dancing in shows and competition; I wished for the toe stand to subvert the masculine virtuosity I was expected to perform, defined by heavy, loud and rapid footwork in hard (noisemaking) Irish dancing shoes. In my solo in the Men in Kilt's performance, I performed multiple toe stands in counterpoint to heavier footwork, further developing the complex masculinity of our performance during Las Vegas Gay Pride.

A discussion of subculture and style provides a helpful platform from which to delve further into ideas of motion, gesture and fashion in dance contexts. A more thorough study of gender and sexuality would come a decade after Hebdige's work with Judith Butler's foundational text, *Gender Trouble: Feminism and the Subversion of Identity* (2006). Butler's famous and widely debated claim, "gender is a social construct", targeted the definition of male and female, and all the attendant power structures, touches of style and meaning that come with gender. While they originally intended the work to be a contribution to Feminist scholarship, the book has come to be considered foundational to Queer theory

---

26 In the '80s and '90s rocks were common for men, but when I entered the competition circuit in the late 2000s a form of hypermasculinity had come to dominate men's competitions and rocks were not in vogue. Orfhlaith Ní Bhriain defines a "rock" as, "[…] executed in front, behind, or to the side. 1. Front Rock Step high on ball of front food with a good arch. Place the back foot behind the front foot, the back instep placed firmly against the front arch. Remain high on the balls of the feet, ankles locked, with no space between your legs, and rock from side to side leaning first into the front food and then to the back foot. This may be repeated three to five counts. When rocking to the right, the left ball is the support. When rocking to the left, the right ball is the support." A brush can be described as, "1. The front foot connects with the floor flicking inwards towards the body. 2. In some regions, a brush is called a Cut."

and Gender studies. Lucas Hilderbrand's Film and Media studies interpretation of the classic film, *Paris is Burning* (Livingston 1989), draws attention to Butler's relationship and reliance on the film, and recounts the criticism they drew from Viviane Namaste in 2000 for not showing adequate concern for the lived experiences of trans people in the film (Hilderbrand 2013). Hilderbrand defends Butler by referencing their later, more "humanizing" readings of the film's community through the lens of "survival".

As someone who has been a guest in the Vogue community and benefited from their teachings, fellowship, love and support, these interpretations are challenging to read. They exemplify the way academia exploits the ideas and even careers of Vogue dancers, while failing to grasp the nature of the community and form as its own system of education, capable of producing knowledge. Scholars often reduce communities and their practice to a struggle for survival in the face of objections from members from the community. Over a decade ago, the Ballroom/House leader Luna Luis Ortiz began a podcast seeking to explore narratives of and about the Ballroom/House community:

> The Luna Show started because I got tired of people referencing Paris is Burning (1990). I felt like, yeah, it's a great film, but now it's dated to me. So I thought, why don't we do something that's a hub of interviews by people who are part of this community now? Also because in *Paris is Burning*, it almost treated us like we had no lives. It was all about the ball. It was all fantasy. There were no professionals; nobody was going to school or to work [laughs]. People were in bed, in their apartment, in the dark putting on makeup, and then— ball! It didn't give roundness to who we are as people. We have lawyers and doctors [...] that are a part of the ballroom scene, why not show some of that? But I guess that wouldn't be interesting. So that's why I wanted to do The Luna Show.
>
> [...] but we're a whole bunch of other things. We're not just ball-walkers; we're part of the community. We have jobs. We go to school. We struggle. We make it. We're artists. So that's

what I wanted instead of "the dream." In *Paris is Burning*, Octavia [St. Laurent]'s dreaming about becoming a model, and then the other part is people are dreaming to become Legendary, a word that you can do nothing with outside of ballroom. Also, interestingly enough, it was around the time that HIV was wiping out the ballroom scene, and they didn't even talk about AIDS in the film. I think one person mentioned it: Venus Xtravaganza said, "I don't wanna get 'the AIDS,'" is how she said it. The other part was, except for Kim Pendavis […], all of those costumes, all of that stuff that we create—that all comes from somewhere, right? There was no highlight that we are these wonderful fashion designers and make-up artists. They didn't show any of that. I always had a problem with that. (VisualAIDS 2015)

Ortiz's critical analysis of the creation and reception of Paris is Burning and their support for the Vogue community is fortunately no longer as marginal as it once was owing to the renewed popularity of Voguing today. There are now numerous artistic, academic and commercial institutions that engage with Ballroom/House and that support members of this community. Nevertheless, public and academic discussions continue to promote narratives that are limited in their scope. I have found that while Ballroom/House community members do face persecution and lack of access, they have not been persecuted solely for the things they have been denied. They also face various forms of oppression for what they do have, namely knowledge. Ballroom/House members have knowledge not only of gender performativity, but also of power and the way it moves through the world. This knowledge is extraordinarily powerful and has the potential to change the odds of a player in the game of capitalism. Butler was not responsible for discovering that gender is a social construct. Rather, they merely articulated in an English academic text a widely-known practice undertaken by, in particular, Trans members of the Ballroom/House community. Vogue, particularly the Old Way, was taught to me as not only a medium for understanding my gender and sexuality (I was a "Butch Queen"), but also as a method and process of conducting personal business, fashion, and even spiritual affairs. I studied with Celso with their hope that I would carry the teachings of Vogue into Irish step dance, and to Ireland. Such is the potential of embodied knowledge.

My own queer interpretations of Irish step dance were enhanced by dancing in the Ballroom/House community. When I met Celso, I knew little of Vogue as a dance form and even less of the Ballroom/House community. At the time, the dance form did not enjoy the popularity it now does with television shows like *RuPaul's Drag Race* (2009), Pose (2018) and *Legendary* (2020). The resource that dancers relied on at that time consisted of YouTube Videos from the late 1990s/2000s, *Paris is Burning* and Chantal Regnault's photography, including the book *Voguing and the House Ballroom Scene of New York, 1989-92* (Regnault 2011). This book was a prized possession for dancers in the Ballroom/House community. Since Celso had asked me to own my Step and my Vogue, I was required to build not just a language of movement, but also, with Celso's guidance, to discover a newfound, deeper connection to Irish culture and tradition through the meeting of Queerness and Irish-ness. There was an understanding that this subculture subverted the idea of Irish dance's "comely young maidens dancing at crossroads".[27] More fundamental, however, was the renewal of Irish-ness and Celtic-ness that came from the willingness to hold this knowledge not just on the body, like the Celtic knot-work dresses of Irish dancing competitions, but within and emanating from the body. Through this process, the technological is connected with the somatic. We shall explore this choreographically in greater detail in the next chapter.

A decade after Butler made their most famous publications, Feminism has guided and shaped our understanding of new materialisms, performativity and post-humanism, providing new methods of understanding subject and object interactions as well

---

27 For a thorough analysis , see Aoife Monks, *Comely Maidens and Celtic Tigers: Riverdance and Global Performance* (London: Goldsmiths, University of London, 2007).

as phenomenology as a whole. While this academic framework could potentially be seen implying a Cartesian detachment of mind from body, it is nonetheless helpful for untangling the layers of this Arts Practice study of Irish step dance and its objects. Karen Barad's writing on "post-human performativity" argues that:

> According to Bohr, the primary epistemological unit is not independent objects with inherent boundaries and properties but rather phenomena. On my agential realist elaboration, phenomena do not merely mark the epistemological inseparably of "observer" and "observed"; rather, phenomena are the ontological inseparability of agentially intra-acting "components." That is, phenomena are ontologically primitive relations—relations with preexisting relate. The notion of intra-action (in contrast to the usual "interaction", which presumes the prior existence of independent entities/relata) represents a profound conceptual shift. (Barad 2003: 815)

In the context of academic philosophy, Barad and other Feminist scholars have challenged human-centric assumptions about how the world works and what it means to produce knowledge. They have sought to de-construct long-standing patriarchies, offering more immediate, practical interpretations of phenomenology. Their concept of "intra-action" informs my understanding of psychometrical "encounter". It envelops encounter's fraught associations with the elite world of art curation so that we may more mindfully engage with it and re-purpose it in dance.

With a more distributed field of analysis, we are more prepared to challenge long-held assumptions on-the-way-the-world-works. When considering the somatic and the technological, Susan Stryker's definition of the somatechnic offers a helpful beginning:

> In 2003 a group of academics at Macquarie University organized a conference on body modification. The aim of the event was to articulate the diverse ways in which all bodies—not simply those that are tattooed or those that have

undergone some sort of transformative surgical procedure—are always already modified. One of the keynote speakers at the conference was Susan Stryker, whose work in the field of transgender studies problematized the "common-sense" understanding of technology, which, at the time, underpinned the dominant model of the transsexual body as either requiring or having undergone technological intervention. Following the conference, Stryker and her colleagues at Macquarie coined the term somatechnics in an attempt to highlight what they saw as the inextricability of soma and techné, of the body (as a culturally intelligible construct) and the techniques (dispositifs and hard technologies) in and through which corporealities are formed and transformed. From the outset, then, somatechnics has addressed and been shaped by transgender issues, and this connection was explicitly articulated at the Transsomatechnics conference held at Simon Fraser University in 2008. (Sullivan 2014: 187)

While affirming an understanding of the post-human, somatechnics also provides a more subtle way of grasping the simple notion that all things in a field are related together. Our bodies and our lived experiences are always already engaged with technology. This relationship can be considered from digital, biological, cultural or political standpoints. When it comes to psychometric theory and dance, somatechnics shows that corporealities are always being created and always evolve from this encounter, and that this is true for everyone. As I will discuss in the next section, Disability studies offers another, more thorough interrogation of the normal versus transformation polemic that it is the goal of somatechnics to challenge.

As Artificial Intelligence (AI) hastens the need to grasp the implications of a curated world ingested for AI models to train on, our understanding of intra-action and the post-human has only grown more complicated. I use Scholar GPT, a ChatGPT marketplace app, to summarize the field of "new materialisms":

"New Materialisms" refers to a contemporary trend in various fields across the humanities and social sciences, including philosophy, feminism, science studies, and environmental studies. This movement re-evaluates the significance of matter and materiality in our understanding of the world, challenging the dominant postmodern focus on language, discourse, and social construction. New Materialisms advocate for a more nuanced approach that considers how material conditions, bodies, and non-human actors contribute to cultural and social phenomena.

By emphasizing the active role of matter in shaping realities and acknowledging the entangled relationships between human and non-human entities, New Materialisms offer a framework for rethinking many foundational assumptions about the world and our place within it. (Accessed 3/29/24)

Having AI re-present new materialist knowledge poses a meta problem in research. In Chapter Five, I will more closely consider AI and its implications for psychometry, intimate violence and impact-driven dance. Jack Halberstam has recently called for a "re-wilding" of Queer studies (Halberstam 2020). Meanwhile ecofeminism, intersectionality and applied research have further expanded the field so that it can confront the crisis of climate change, global inequality and the human rights crisis. I incorporate this lineage into dance practice as I explore Irish step dance through the lens of impact-driven dance. Impact-driven dance, when it is situated within the communities that shaped it, implies a posthumanist knowledge system. Psychometry views this complex system through the dancer and the dance, action and counteraction, object and subject. It implies that the dancer comes to know the world through an embodied choreo-language in the process of creating the dance.

My experience as a dancer with disabilities learning from and working with other dancers with disabilities informed my Step&Vogue methodology. It led me to develop psychometric perspectives that would inspire my first major work, *The Querist*, allowing encounter to create real meetings out of objects through lived experience. Understanding the somatechnic in psychometric dance brings us back to autoethnography to reveal the personal experience of intra-actions temporally, kinetically and somatically.

The Disabled: Stepping in Vogue at the Blue Teapot

For my first class at the Blue Teapot with the Teacups, a group consisting of adults with intellectual disability undertaking their first year of study in a three-year professional training program for actors, I requested that the students bring gloves. This prompted commotion and curiosity from the apprentice actors (soon-to-be dancers), their families and carers. In the summer of 2016, Rachel Parry, a friend and colleague studying intellectual disability and dance at the National University of Ireland, Galway had suggested I teach Vogue at the Blue Teapot. I had never taught a class in Vogue before and was unsure whether I was the right candidate. In this case the need for a dance teacher seemed clear, and they were looking for something outside mainstream contemporary dance. Rachel, I believe, spotted an opportunity for shared understanding and empathy.

It occurred to me that the best way to begin the series of six classes was chirologically; if you want a quick way to learn about hands and how they move, put on a pair of gloves. After a warm-up and a couple videos explaining what Vogue is and who does it, I had the dancers sit in two rows of chairs facing one chair at the front of the class. One-at-time, I asked them to bring their gloves and sit in the chair facing the rest of the room. I would ask them to put on and take off the gloves. The awkwardness, complexity or indeed grace of the hands became obvious. It was riveting; the simplest of tasks in dance can often be the most engaging for audiences. Next, I wanted to help the performers to find what animates hands into gesture. I asked them once again to put on and take off the gloves, but this time they were to mimic selling the gloves to the class without saying a word. The assignment was open to the actor's interpretation as long as they found ways to convince us to buy their pair of gloves. Out of all the possible motivations for putting on and taking off a pair of gloves, this was important to me from a fashion perspective as it is what clothing models do: lunge, contort and exercise ease and beauty in such a way that it makes others want to have what they have. This was part of my education in Vogue: coming to understand the basic modeling poses, and why we do them. I felt the best way for the neophyte dancers to learn what I had learned from Vogue was not just to mirror choreography, but to discover in their own bodies how they would "choreonavigate" capitalism. Lastly, I gave them a more provocative assignment; they were to use the gloves to sell themselves. I left this completely open to their own interpretation, and I offer no analysis of this here. The room remained silent and focused throughout the exercise as choreographic, theatrical play came to life.

This exercise was borne of my understanding of new materialisms and the academic theory's roots in, ongoing relationship with (and reliance on) Vogue/Ballroom/House. My goal was not to turn my students into Vogue dancers, but to show them the care I had felt in the Ballroom/House community and to share some of their methods. The glove exercise and other fashion-based tasks I assigned them were intended to support both dancers and spectators alike to confront ideas of normalcy, something Lennard Davis claims is central to Disability Studies (Davis 2013). The classroom's awareness of the tasks I assigned the dancers and the knowledge that the dancers were living with intellectual disability (they were aware of each other's disabilities as well as mine) unsettled expectations around normalcy, allowing each dancer to meet that expectation on their own terms. As capitalism is always re-inventing and re-asserting itself in "new markets" (new demographics previously overlooked or excluded), these fashion tasks (a choreographed HTE) were intended to encapsulate the complex relationship of theater and performance with capitalism as a medium for the sale of ideas, style and even people as sex workers or chattel. The actor is invited to perform the most common task demanded of them under capitalism, to sell something: to get others to want or feel something in particular. How the dancer meets, refuses to meet, is unable to meet or re-invents that meeting reflects the ability of Vogue to help the dancer re-negotiate the capitalist's contract on the body, i.e., that it is for sale and it is your privilege that determines what you are selling. In the case of the Teacups, any questions concerning their success at the tasks only served to further underline the point; witnesses are needed to the spectacle of the performance.

My classes with the "cups" were extended for the entire semester. I was also asked to teach a short Vogue dance course with the professional acting company, the "pots". I did not go into the Blue Teapot thinking that my work there would influence my doctoral research or be a part of it. However, after the fact I recognized that they informed my research and deepened my understanding. Davis's seminal work on disability confirmed what I had learned from other professional educators and artists working with performers living with intellectual disability, namely that we should "[…] focus not so much on the construction of disability as on the construction of normalcy" and that "[…] the 'problem' is not the person with disabilities; the problem is the way that normalcy is constructed to create the 'problem' of the disabled person." (Davis 2013: 1) Disability studies taught me how to de-center the norm (or at least how to know what the norm is and that it is in the center) by showing me how the world can be made accessible to anyone. Regardless of whether or not the world is made accessible to those living with disabilities in the way we expect it to be, it is always accessed by them all the same. To learn this is to receive a tremendous gift of knowledge. If we were to allow our public spaces to be re-negotiated the world would become all the more accessible to everyone and thereby all the more interesting and welcoming.

Working at the Blue Teapot and learning from scholars and artists in Disability Studies helped me to recognize and better understand my own para-ambulatory relationship to Irish step dance. I am completely deaf in my right ear. My hearing disability presents a great many challenges and as a lifelong musician has tended to make ensemble performance inaccessible to me (another way of saying that I am not wanted in those spaces). In many cases, this has altered my career trajectory. As a harper I was welcome to play in Irish traditional music sessions at local pubs, but the harp sits on my right shoulder, I am deaf in my right ear and the other musicians typically play quite loud. As a result I could not hear my own playing. It was too burdensome for myself and others to work out accommodations, so this career path remained closed to me despite a lifetime in Irish traditional music and my undergraduate degree in classical Western music. This may be an unfortunate reality in the world of live music performance, however percussive dance's evolution into a musical product spreads the problem. The earliest references to percussive dance do not position the art form as a musical product, that would come later through the "Ensoniment" of the Western world:

> As there was an Enlightenment, so too was there an "Ensoniment." A series of conjectures among ideas, institutions, and practices rendered the world audible in new ways and valorized new constructs of hearing and listening. Between 1750 and 1925, sound itself became an object and a domain of thought and practice, where it had previously been conceptualized in terms of particular idealized instances like voice or music. Hearing was reconstructed as a physiological process, a kind of receptivity and capacity based upon physics, biology, and mechanics. Through techniques of listening, people harnessed, modified, and shaped their powers of auditory perception in the service of rationality. In the modern age, sound and hearing were reconceptualized, objectified, imitated, transformed, reproduced, commodified, mass-produced, and industrialized. To be sure, the transformation of sound and hearing took well over a century. It is not that people woke up one day and found everything suddenly different. Changes in sound, listening, and hearing happened

> bit by bit, place by place, practice by practice, over a long period of time... (Sterne 2003: 2)

While no body of scholarship exists to chronicle the history of footwear in percussive dance, I argue that an "Ensoniment" of percussive dance included the forced wearing of wooden shoes and the gradual removal of soft, earthen floors from domestic spaces. Later, American Tap dance's metal taps and Irish step dance's nails, fiberglass tips and the world of sound recording accelerated the process of turning dance into music. Today this sight-meets-sound trope is enshrined in New York Times dance critic Brian Seibert's history of American Tap dance in *What the Eye Hears: A History of Tap Dancing* (2015). As previously discussed, cognitive metaphors influence not only knowledge production, but also practice. In Irish step dance contexts the sound-based narrative has become so dominant that some dancers have abandoned the practice of looking at the audience with their backs to the musicians—the custom for centuries—and prefer instead to look at the musicians with their side or back facing the audience (Gareiss 2017). For me as an Irish step dancer this new stage direction is not only unnecessary (watching a fiddler play does not help me with my hearing disability), it introduces new patriarchal dynamics in the dance as in my experience the majority of Irish traditional musicians have been men and the majority of Irish traditional step dancers have been women. As an Irish step dancer, this musical imperative supplants the dancers physical, felt and intimate agency.

The supremacy of sound problematizes my partial deafness by making me guilty of the greatest sin possible in Irish step dance: falling out of time. To compete in the CLRG's world championships and not be disqualified I would have to develop new ways of "hearing" the music. In the dance, I found remediation by going further into feeling, as well as by changing my understanding of what it was I was listening for. The silences between notes became just as meaningful as the notes themselves. Total deafness in one ear means being unable to hear the direction of any sound. In the same way that depth perception comes by seeing with two eyes, two ears enable listeners to tell from which direction a friend's greeting, an ambulance or gunshot is coming. To deal with this problem on stage as an Irish step dancer, my sense of the feeling of the music has shifted. When people say they are "feeling the music" they mean they are hearing it and reacting to it emotionally. I do this as well, but at the same time I quite literally feel the vibrations of the music through my skin and so I can better dance with it and meet ableist expectations.

Later when I began to read volumes of "gypsy science"[28] I found surprising comfort in a study that revealed a genetic propensity in Hungarian Roma for hearing impairment (Schrauwen et al. 2019). Around the same time I met an elder Hungarian Roma/Sinti dancer with a hearing disability who has become part of my *kumpania* (community). She in turn taught me about legendary Flamencas[29] Antoñita Singla ("La Singla"), who is deaf, and Micaela Flores Amaya ("La Chunga"),[30] who was known for dancing barefoot—choosing to grasp the ground in an art form famous for thunderous footwork. As I engaged with my Arts Practice research and came to understand my place within a heritage and history of deaf and hard of hearing Roma and Sinti dancers, I came to understand my somatic Irish step dance not just as a coping mechanism, but as a reason to dance; I found embrace in the Irish traditional music that flows through me. The process of Arts Practice research and methods of indigenous autoethnography deployed in this project also worked as intended; they helped me delight in the invention of academic frameworks for hearing-disabled dance that in turn guided me to an ancestral belonging I had previously been unaware of. Given the prominent role of the Hungarian Roma in world histories of percussive dances, I have since developed an imagined ancient origin of

---

28 I am referring to the heavily-funded, ongoing research to genetically study and classify the Roma which has origins in Nazi science. I will cover this more in the upcoming section, "The Romungro".

29 Women who dance Flamenco.

30 In Roma and Sinti communities nicknames are common and they are very common among the Gitanos, Calé and Zincailli.

percussive dance; it is a dance of the hearing disabled who are not as interested in the audible qualities of their movements as they are in nourishing their heightened sense of touch. As I investigate impact-driven dance, I hope to open the field of percussive dance inviting musicians and dancers alike to the sensations of feeling, touch and the physically intimate.

While the relationship between my disability and Irish step dance are certainly of personal interest, a somatechnical application of Disability Studies will demonstrate that we are all aided by technology and innovation to accomplish tasks that we could not have done otherwise. For example, headphones have helped to normalize deafness in public spaces, with more sophisticated headphones such as the AirPod Pros improving public understanding of spatial hearing. Spatial hearing was previously a priority only for wearers of hearing aids, especially the relay-type hearing aids (one ear to the other) that I wear. Headphones offer sound and communication on more personal, customizable terms for those with and without hearing disabilities alike. On most competitive Irish dance stages, sound is also mediated by architectural and electrical means which affect the dancer's ability to engage with their music and the musician's sense of their own sound. The experience of disability reveals a great deal about intimate violence and how different people experience it in impact-driven dance. However, these intra-actions are not without emotion. Traumatic associations are imperative when considering the psychometrical touch of impact-driven dance's past.

The Traumatized: Trauma Exposure and Encounter

In the spring of 2013 I realized I needed help. I was turning thirty and with the state my life was in, I realized things were not working out. By some grace I saw that at least part of the problem was inside me and I needed other people with different ways of thinking to guide me to a better life. I enlisted mental health expertise.

A couple of months later I was in the middle of a psychiatric evaluation when the doctor was called out of the room. I glanced at her evaluation and saw scribbled:

> *Diagnosis: anxiety, possible OCD, post-traumatic stress disorder—most likely since childhood*

After the rigorous questioning I had endured, my head was spinning with thoughts, questions and memories that I did not know whether to laugh about, cry over or keep to myself. To see written on paper such a simple and abrupt description of "me" was both offensive and oddly comforting. I believed that the field of psychology constituted a mixture of vague philosophical diagnosis, sympathy and common-sense advice. This smattering of terms from the DSM-V[31] combined with my care provider's approach to addressing my situation suggested a cool clarity, a firm tone and a sober examination of past experience giving hope of freedom from disorder. I also believed that, as I sat in the room, I would simply be regurgitating my personal history; this would take some work on my part. When she returned to the room, amid my confusion I heard the word "remission." My treatment had begun.

My program was based on the research of Marylène Cloitre at New York University Langone Medical Center and was composed

---

31 The American Psychiatric Association publishes a dictionary of mental illnesses, the latest edition is titled the DSM-5. See Diagnostic and Statistical Manual of Mental Disorders: DSM-5 (American Psychiatric Publishing, Inc, 2013).

of two parts (Cloitre 2006). Over the next several months I underwent a process that is often applied to PTSD patients as the first part of their therapy: a treatment called STAIR (Skills Training in Affect and Interpersonal Regulation). This would help me to stop identifying with the darkness and to learn how to walk out of the shadow, into the light. The second part of the therapy, the core of PTSD treatment called "exposure" therapy, would allow me to see what had blocked out the sun in the first instance, and how I could reasonably avoid getting caught underneath it again. STAIR was informed by up-to-date research in Cognitive Behavioral Therapy designed to help patients "[…improve] in three specifically targeted problem domains: affect regulation problems, interpersonal skills deficits and PTSD symptoms" (Cloitre et al. 2002: 1067). This ensured that when the exposure part of the therapy began, I would have the skills necessary to process whatever happened to me.

Exposure therapy consists of numerous methods. One method advocated for survivors of childhood abuse is "Narrative Story Telling". In this approach patients are instructed:

> You will engage in the emotional processing of your abuse experiences by repeated narration of the events of your early life. The goal will be to help you make meaningful connections between your feelings and your experiences in a safe and supportive environment. Staying with these memories rather than running away from them can be very distressing at first, but over time it will help decrease the anxiety and fear that are associated with them. In addition, this process will allow you to identify the ways in which the present is different from the past, freeing you to behave and think differently. It will also provide you with a life narrative, which will allow you to take a long view of your life and see your trauma as only one of the many possible experiences that you may have. (Cloitre 2006: 126)

The goal of this method is to give the patient an opportunity to identify the trauma so that they can learn to no longer identify with it. Patients do not write, read, record and listen back to their traumas in order to reinforce their sense of victimhood or identity as a trauma survivor, but to bring them to a recognition of the facts and details of the trauma that they were previously denied or that they were not able to understand at the time. This in turn enables them to discover who the person is who experienced and continues to experience the trauma. Exposure therapy can take place in a group setting, or it can involve visiting places where the trauma occurred or handling objects related to the trauma, such as clothing. With each encounter the pain is better understood. The month I spent undergoing narrative story telling as a form of exposure therapy was one of the hardest times in my life. The result, however, was astonishing: the trauma—which hitherto lurked behind inappropriate jokes at parties, unhealthy habits and memories playing on a horrific loop during waking and sleeping hours—ended. The incidents my therapist and I had identified as core to my narrative story telling experience were still upsetting to discuss. However, my mind, heart and body know that the trauma is over. I also know that I have the skills to avoid these situations in the future.

I began my research project the first year of my master's degree (2013–14). As my PTSD treatment progressed, I could not help but consider my lessons on trauma in the light of an Irish Studies and Atlantic world perspective. This meant applying my personal experience of trauma and PTSD treatment to collective—shared, intergenerational and cultural—trauma.

When observing the spread of a contagious disease, an obvious place to start looking is among the healthcare professionals who treat the infected. Similarly, in treating PTSD the term "shared trauma" is often used to define trauma that is contracted as a result of treating PTSD sufferers. Especially when dealing with large-scale disaster, the care of healthcare workers becomes difficult as "intrapsychic, interpersonal, community, and societal" factors come to influence the traumatic impact of events (Tosone 2012). Yael Danieli in his study of multigenerational trauma notes the "conspiracy of silence" among Holocaust survivors, observing that "Both intrapsychically and interpersonally protective, silence is profoundly destructive, for it attests to the person's, family's, society's, community's, and nation's inability to integrate the trauma" (Marsella et al. 2007: 66). The ability to incorporate the world's most profound traumas into one's own life is essential to recovery from PTSD. Danieli observes that within the intergenerational setting, there are:

> At least three *intrafamilial* components (a) the parent's trauma, its parameters, and the offspring's own relationship to it; (b) the nature and extent of the conspiracy of silence surrounding the trauma and its aftermath; and (c) their parent's *posttrauma adaptational styles*. (Ibid.: 69)

Unless pro-active steps are taken, these processes of trauma transmission are likely to be repeated generation after generation.

Several studies support the genetic transmission of learned behavior, including trauma. An article published in *Nature Neuroscience* describes an experiment whereby mice were conditioned to fear the odor of cherries. Their results showed that the second and third generation offspring also demonstrated a traumatic reaction to the odor and that "the behavior and structural alterations were inherited and were not socially transmitted from the F0 (first) generation" (Dias and Ressler 2013). The implication is that for humans, similar fear-based reactions, such as PTSD, can be encoded into DNA and passed on to subsequent generations without any modeling from parents or grandparents.

It is difficult not to see the connection between intergenerational and shared trauma producing broader cultural patterns: PTSD behavior becomes normalized behavior then learned behavior and ultimately cultural behavior. Cathy Caruth's *Unclaimed Experience: Trauma, Narrative, and History* is a foundational text in traumatology which has had widespread influence in literary studies and beyond. This work applies clinical expertise to the study of literature, history, philosophy and public memory (1996). In the last twenty years arts scholarship and therapy has become increasingly interested in the subject of trauma and its treatment across cultural contexts. In this project I wish to return to the psychometric encounter and its connection to curation, that is the organization of tangible objects that bear traumatic histories. In a "trauma-led" society, especially one with marginalized communities heavily impacted by violence, the psychometric encounter is expanded by dance's capacity to feel hurt when we touch something, an act which, over time, facilitates awareness. When I was attending a Flamenco *tablao* (a place where Flamenco is performed), someone at my table explained that they were learning to sing *cante* (Flamenco singing) and joked about how all the songs they had to learn were woefully tragic. As he joked about dying donkeys and losing your hut, his comments were met with laughter. The only other Romani person at the *tablao* was on the stage playing guitar, so there was no point in explaining to him why the artform might embody the past horrors inflicted on the Roma and Sinti. For me as a non-Spanish Roma, cante is like hearing my cousins' songs of struggles. For most gadje, Flamenco is a sexy form of escapism, an entertainment and, for the ambitious, a way to get in shape.[32] For the Spanish Roma on the other hand, cante exists as a form of "narrative story telling" that carries within it historical and contemporary trauma. I argue that this also applies to the dance. In each *zapateado* (footsound), as foot meets ground, so much trauma spills out that it is heard.

As I speak of the human–technological encounter and its propensity for intimate violence, impact-driven dance curates these watery, emotional "aquapelagic assemblages" (Joseph and Varino 2017) of shared, intergenerational and cultural traumas through and beyond time. As I will discuss in Chapter Five, the

---

32 While the Roma may enjoy their sexuality, fitness or amusement in dance, this lives alongside the processing of collective and personal trauma. For most non-Roma dancing Flamenco and other Romani dance forms, they have no awareness that such trauma exists and in my experience, no interest in respecting that lived experience and how it has informed the artform they are enjoying. Our arts are appropriated as an exotic escape and intellectual fantasy for the non-Roma.

rhythms of the impact-driven dancer create new meaning by way of phraseology, style and self-expression.

The Romungro:[33] Kalipen and Romani Techno-Witchcraft

In 2017, after learning about Queer, Trans, Feminist, Black, Indigenous, Disabled and Irish communities, cultures and knowledge production, I thought that if I started talking about Romani identity I would be able to have similar exciting, engaging and challenging academic conversations around Romani Dance and identity. Instead, what I have experienced and continue to endure since then is the violence of a human–technological apparatus used by the non-Roma to appropriate from us and ultimately eliminate us. As I opened up about my Romani identity I discovered:

- There are no degree-granting Romani Studies programs anywhere in the Western Hemisphere;
- No universities with which to study my native, critically endangered language, Romungro, or any other Roma or Sinti dialect;
- Not one single department of dance in the world calls the dances they teach Romani or Sinti dance;
- Non-Roma academics and artists would not allow me to use the term Romani Dance or Sinti Dance;
- The largest, oldest and most powerful funded body of the study of Romani people is still run by wealthy, white Englishmen (the Gypsy Lore Society);
- The Gypsy Lore Society and many other non-Roma in Romani Studies continue to carry out racist Nazi eugenic research in

---

33 I am of the Romungre sub-group of the Roma.

their search for the pure gypsy;[34]

- Several senior Romani scholars are exiled from their home countries for simply being Romani;
- I am the only Romani Dance scholar in North America;
- In Europe are the only two Romani Studies programs;
- 80% of the Roma in Europe live in poverty, often without clean water, shelter or healthcare;[35]
- So-called gypsy laws abound in the United States, including in my home state of New York;
- Centuries of British and American legislation were designed to erase us (Ostendorf 2020);

---

34 The Nazis promoted eugenics by various means including genetic testing. Studies are still regularly carried out and heavily funded by the non-Roma to genetically test the identity of Romani people. For an example see Adnan, Atif, Allah Rakha, Hayder Lazim, Shahid Nazir, Wedad Saeed Al-Qahtani, Maha Abdullah Alwaili, Sibte Hadi, and Chuan-Chao Wang. "Are Roma People Descended from the Punjab Region of Pakistan: A Y-Chromosomal Perspective." *Genes* 13, no. 3 (March 17, 2022): 532. https://doi.org/10.3390/genes13030532.

35 "80% of Roma interviewed remain at risk of poverty compared with an EU average of 17%, no change from before. 22% live in households with no tap water and 33% have no indoor toilet. But overall, Roma living in poor housing fell from 61% in 2016 to 52% now", see FRA, "Roma in 10 European Countries."

For the last seven years I mistakenly thought that if I pointed these things out to other scholars at major conferences that people would want this to change. Instead, professional dancers, teachers and senior scholars said to me:

- "We don't even know if the gypsies are real."
- "Aren't you part of that [insert Jewish anti-semitic conspiracy]?"
- "Roma? You mean the city, that's a made up name for a people."
- "You have stolen your culture from white people."
- "You don't have a culture, you have stolen your culture from Black people."[36]

It has been painful to hear these statements from academics who genuinely believe they are advocates for social justice and political progress. While there is much that can be said about these statements and their effect on me, I would like to focus here on the impact of oppression and how the silencing of that oppression has shaped my dance and this project. First, when discussing Romani Dance it is critical to understand that you are engaging with a forbidden, submerged field of study. Most music and dance scholars would deny that such a thing as Roma or Sinti dance, music or performing art exists. This means that in dance theater and academia I do not dance with the support of institutional bodies, since those bodies do not recognize that my body exists. I dance with hopelessness. This is one way in which impact is silenced. To make sure I experience silence in isolation, the academy divides the study of Romani across regional dividing

---

36 Taken from my journal, each of these are real statements that have been said to me in response to me simply claiming my Romani identity and, in particular, claiming Romani agency and authorship in dance history. I have unpacked statements such as these at conferences, see Rosemary Cisneros and Russell Patrick Brown, "Forbidden Movement : Historical and Contemporary Ant i-Gypsyism in Dance and the Emergence of Romani Dance Studies," in *New Mobilities "on the Turn"* (Dance Studies Association, The Place, London, 2023).

lines that reflect gadje racial and ethnic nationalism. This has a powerful effect on how Romani culture is perceived. For one, it suggests that Roma and Sinti people do not work together to understand shared silences and impacts and to support one another's exploration of our own rich, varied choreo-destiny. Furthermore, many gadje have used genocide as a method of silencing. The very concept of the Bohemian artist, foundational to the development of artistic practice in the west, was based on the Czech Roma, who were called Bohemians. This was fairly well known until the Holocaust almost completely removed the Bohemian Roma from existence. This act of genocide gave the non-Roma the freedom to appropriate Bohemianism in the second half of the 20th century unencumbered by the existence of real Bohemians. While I imagine most non-Roma self-proclaimed "Bohemians" do not support genocide, the silence caused by ethnically and racially-motived mass murder allowed their voices to be amplified. With no reparations having been awarded to the Roma since the end of World War II and with the continued refusal of scholarship to recognize Romani agency in the arts, we can draw a relationship between genocide and the ways that non-Roma profit at the expense of the Roma and Sinti. The enormity of the crime makes the obvious invisible, suggesting that perhaps some impacts are so loud we cannot hear them. Following these two observations on silence, the last point I would like to make is that as a Romani impact-driven dancer, my dance is not based on the progressive assumption that our day of justice will come. I do not wish to suggest there are not Roma and non-Roma alike working for Roma liberation since indeed there are. What I mean is that these silences, which are so much larger than myself, have a very real impact on the way I dance and how people hear that dance. I explore this phenomenon in greater detail in my second major work, *AngelAI*.

The Roma are not alone in being oppressed, and intersectionalism has at times created opportunities for solidarity and prompted some interesting turns in research, such as in the case of Noémie Ndiaye's groundbreaking work on African and Romani representation in Renaissance drama (Ndiaye 2022). Ndiaye's work is characterized by award-winning archival research, innovative theoretical analysis, as well as kindness and "respect" for "people from diverse cultures" as described by Rokia Traoré in her song "Sé Dan" (2016). This unfortunately is not the norm in the field, and few gadje scholars have the anti-racist training sufficient to tackle popular representations of Romani culture while hardly any have the competency to speak on Romani culture itself. The most egregious outcome from this lack of education is the unchallenged promotion of the core gypsyist37 belief that Roma and Sinti people have no culture of their own. The complete absence of the Romani and Sinti languages from almost all studies of our performance culture confirms this. For example, Meira Goldberg's award-winning monograph on *Sonidos Negros: On the Blackness of Flamenco* (2018) nowhere addresses the experience of Blackness in Romani contexts. Goldberg's groundbreaking study of Blackness in dance performance in Europe (a subject seldom studied) is overshadowed by her failure to incorporate a Romani perspective on Blackness. Not even to mention that the Romani name for the Spanish Roma is *Calé*, or Caló (the Spanish Romani dialect), which is the plural noun for black or dark-skinned people is to deny our language, the way we have been racially classified and our perspectives and practices. Kalipen (Blackness or darkness) as I have defined it in this work presents a vast topic rich with meaning, history and sacred significance for Romani people. However, it is silenced in non-Roma contexts since progressive research has consistently failed to call out Nazi ideals. In most gadje scholarship Romani people exist only as a fantasy, a foil and

---

37 Anti-gypsyism refers to practices, beliefs and institutionalized prejudices and discriminations designed to oppress Romani people. I often just call this gypsyism, as "gypsy" is a misnomer and a racial slur and I do not know any other Roma or Sinti who use it except internally. Exonymic names for the Roma and Sinti such as *Gitano* (Spanish) or *Zigeuner* (German) have been reappropriated in some contexts, and for Roma and Sinti people this is seldom a source of conflict. For the gadje, however, the variety of names for the Roma and Sinti is confusing and is often believed to be a cause of infighting.

an escape for the gadje from the systems they have built, benefit from and all the same feel oppressed by.

While the situation in dance studies is hopeless, Margareta Matache's work on the Harvard Romani Studies Program has supported unprecedented research on the Romani experience in America. It has been healing for my family to participate in this research process ("Romani Realities in the United States: Breaking the Silence, Challenging the Stereotypes." 2020). In Irish contexts, universities have increased representation of and support for Romani and Traveller people in recent years. While there are many differences between Travellers and Roma, their cultures and experience with social justice issues are comparable. Oein DeBhairduin's *Why the Moon Travels* sent shockwaves through the Irish literary community, highlighting the contribution of Travellers to Irish culture. DeBhairduin targeted the Irish Folklore Commission for taking sources from and failing to attribute them to Irish Travellers (DeBhairduin 2020). Sandra Joyce's research into Traveller song I found enlightening for the care and respect with which it approaches ethnographic research (Joyce 2015). Despite all this, the centuries-old presence of the Roma in Ireland remains, for the most part, unstudied. As in most of Europe, there exist studies of human rights, social work, public health and education covering Europe's largest ethnic racial minority. However, when it comes to the performing arts there is hardly any research that has been carried out by Romani people or that suggests any anti-racist training on the part of the researcher.

I share these truths as they are part of my experience, and they have a direct impact on my steps. As an elder in my community said to me, "Our people have endured while entire countries and empires have risen and fallen." This perspective implies a different sense of kali (time), one not ridden with the belief that all will be well so long as we buy the latest social justice smokescreens from the neoliberal marketplace of human suffering, one based around the preservation and transfer of values from generation to generation. It is less about educating the gadje, who are unlikely to understand or care about these issues and even less likely acknowledge the scale of their theft from our culture, and more about supporting Romani people such that our existence and survival does not depend on or center around gadje constructions even as they are impacted by them.

The word *Kalipen* denotes the ancient Sanskrit association between time and darkness. I take the idea of *Kalipen* further to evoke Blackness embodied in the traditional Romani worship of Sara Kali, our patron saint. I evoke the Kalipen of the Roma not to create an exotic sense of time or otherness, but to represent our own agency and right to feel, to be. I use the word Kalipen to capture the black and brown physical expression (skin, hair, eyes) of my Romani family. While the impact of gypsyism and anti-Romani racism varies from the painfully loud to the cruelly silent, the collision against my *Romanipen* (Romani-ness) is what taught me about intimate violence most acutely. As I psychometrically touch my Irish dancing hard shoes or my bare feet to the floor, I realized something my identities had taught me: that the most powerful resistance and truth I could find was to simply just *feel the impact*. This meant intimately experiencing the moments before, during and after the violence of my choreography. The dance thereby became a kind of exposure therapy, each moment a chance to confront a violent history that is being continually played out today, and to find out who I am within it. It was necessary to let this violent history echo throughout my being, rather than to cover over the pain with virtuosity or stereotype, such as when people would say to my family at *feisanna* (Irish dancing festivals) that we did not look Irish before I would go on to win my competition. On the contrary, feeling the impact meant feeling what it is to be me, to be Romani and finding that the more I meet the rhythms of ancestors with precision and fullness of being, the more I transcend these rotten times. This would change everything. In my exploration of the psychometric in dance, I came to realize that I was not fighting to make others believe that I knew the history of an object simply by touching it like some fortune-telling gypsy (which I am and which my family has been for generations), but that I was insisting on the right to feel, to express intimacy for others and intimacy for myself as I touched the world. My psychometric perspective as informed by Romanipen aims to reclaim the Romani experience in an interconnected, mind-body-spirit totality.

When I began my research I did not expect to find any of this. In fact I began my research in 2013 with my own white fragility struggling against my training in Black and Afro-diasporic dance forms. However, in the course of my studies I gradually became convinced that there is a Blackness within Irish step dance. Two texts fundamentally changed how I understood Irish step dance and percussive dance: *Black dance in London, 1730-1850: innovation, tradition and resistance* by Rodreguez King-Dorset (2010) and *Afro-Mexico: dancing between myth and reality* Anita Gonzalez (2010). Not only did these texts help me to better contextualize my understanding of nationality as it is shaped by race and ethnicity. They also facilitated a more nuanced understanding of how dance moved around the Atlantic world and beyond. I have never found evidence that jigs, hornpipes and reels emerged from any kind of pure white European culture, moving East to West. Instead, I found that these things evolved with the input of communities of color in Europe and beyond.

Over time, my understanding of Afro-diasporic dance expanded alongside my understanding of Blackness as lived experience and as a saleable commodity for white people in the Atlantic world. This process required patience and the acceptance that there are certain things I would never understand fully, such as the experiences of communities to which I do not belong. However, I had to overcome my caution as it is imperative to keep asking and learning. This work took an unexpected turn when I, outside my research, began speaking publicly about my Romani identity. In time I came to discover the hidden-in-plain-sight histories and practices of Romani Dance, and to recognize our kalipen and Romanipen in that dance. I was inspired by *Black Performance Theory* (DeFrantz and Gonzalez 2014) and its view of BPT as an area of study rich in history and meaning. I carried this work's method of inquiry into Critical Romani Studies and Romani Dance Studies. When I cite kalipen I also cite the BPT that helped me to define Romanipen in gadje, Anglophone academic contexts. Meanwhile, I have had conversations with Black dance scholars and other Romani Dance scholars and artists as a means of exploring the intersections of Romani and African identities, practices, origins and communities. I aim to continue this work into the future in an effort to find out where our cultures intersect in spaces unmediated by whiteness and other hegemonies.

The last identity and lived experience I draw on to characterize the psychometric encounter is that of the Romani Techno-witch. The Roma Futurism Manifesto, written by Romani activist and theater artist Mihaela Drăgan, states: "Roma Futurism is an artistic current that creates interactions of Roma culture with technology and witchcraft. It combines elements of science fiction, Roma history, fantasy, Roma subjectivity, magical realism, creative technologies with magical practices and rituals of healing" ("ROMA FUTURISM" 2020). Combining a curatorial ERIAC approach with the Romani Art revolution alongside inspiration from Afro-futurism, Roots work and conjure feminism, Roma Futurism re-asserts Romani historical relationships with performance, technology and spiritual awareness, innovation and self-determinism. Among other things, the Roma brought puppetry to Europe and furthered the arts of circus and court jester-ing, Spanish Romani scholar Miguel Ángel Vargas also identifies the role of Romani innovation and agency in the creation of modern performance as we know it. The concept of Roma futurism has helped me understand the forms of intuition and technological innovation taught to me by my mother. I am connected to a long lineage of metalworking ancestors, as well as 20th-century innovators such as Charlie Chaplin (Romanichal) and Nikola Tesla (Vlacchia). When applied to the present research, Romani techno-witchcraft allows us to understand how, at least in a Romani context, our human–technological encounters may also be metaphysical.

The practice of Romani Techno-Witchcraft carries my identities further into my dance, into time, into kalipen. Each snap, clap, tap, wrap, slap and stomp re-orders, re-invents and encircles time through the magic of rhythm, which can be defined as a hyperchronic re-ordering of human–technological encounter into a new structure and order of time and space. Rhythm and its reflexive relationship with gestural patterns, impatient tapping and human expression becomes the construct of the HTE and the psychometric turn upon it set in motion, a process both through and beyond time and space. It is at the core of my two major works. More broadly, these rhythms create impact-driven dance. The ability of dancers to move through these collisions and re-order them in time constitutes a language of time, of change.

Summary

In defining psychometry, I favor the right to feel, which has so often been described as magic or as something exotically sexual to those who have lost or do not value the ability to feel the world around them. I favor the experience of the interaction, and the impact on the body, and the body's impact on the intra-action, even the impact itself. What strikes skeptics as sacrilegious or academically suspect about psychometry is not the fact that someone could know something about an object by merely touching it, but that someone could feel anything at all when touching objects and claim that these potentially messy feelings matter. For impact-driven dancers, what we feel when we touch *matters* (gives form to matter). When we claim ownership of this feeling there is sobriety, when we understand how this affects us we gain knowledge and when we dance this we become awakened to our creative potential.

New Materialism is central to how I approach my choreography and this research. Psychometry is my contribution to this field. It is not just what we know in object intra-relations that matters, it is what we feel and become that matters. This chapter began with several definitions of the psychometric taken from Spiritualist contexts, before recounting my experience as a gay male Irish dancer re-acquainting himself with the form from a queer perspective before developing practice as a guest in the Royal Iconic House of LaBeija. My account of these lived experiences foregrounded Feminist, Queer and Trans theoretical perspectives on the post-human performative, the somatechnic and what these might mean for our understanding of technology and the human–technological encounter.

My own experiences with disability and work as a dance instructor to other dancers with disabilities both similar and different from my own provided me with the tools to understand HTE from multiple perspectives and gave me the choreographic methods to access them. In the meeting of gloves, fashions and the movement of power through style my definition of a psychometric theoretical perspective found a further practical application. Trauma studies and therapeutic processes of exposure to objects and their associated traumatic histories provided greater insight into the disruptive forces of impact-driven dance, showing how the art form can act as a form of intergenerational trauma therapy.

Lastly, Romani Techno-witchcraft illuminates how rhythmic choreographic invention can serve as a force of agency in the re-ordering of disruptive technologies as time is reconstructed. This agency is built on the right to feel our experience, even as they and we are being erased. I invoke psychometry as a theory in dance practice, using both lived and theoretical perspectives to contextualize my approach to Irish step dance.

CHAPTER FOUR:

The Querist

[A jig, a side step leading with the right leg]
Cut heel and toe, and heel and toe and
Heel and toe, heel and toe and
Jump, kick, hop back-234
Hop, hop back, hop back-234

Words on Caution

Before I introduce this next chapter and the second half of this thesis, I would like to take a moment to speak on the personal challenges, risks and faults that come about in the course of autoethnographic Arts Practice research. Autoethnographic Arts Practice research documents not only the researcher's practice but also their own self and the things they experience during their research process. Incorporating the traumatic histories of impact-driven dance and coming to terms with my ancestral connection to these histories caused me a serious degree of distress.[38] This project constitutes a form a meta self-inquiry which in hindsight I would only recommend with caution. When I originally proposed this research I did not know that I would take so strongly to autoethnography or that it would so effectively support my doctoral work, and neither did my original supervisor. I was also not aware of the personal implications of Roma slavery and

---

38 Conversely my personal relationship to the matter could be seen as predisposing me to better understand and tolerate the difficult feelings and thoughts that arose from it. I am not interested in whether someone can handle their research, but whether they have thought through the impact the work may have on their personhood. I did not do this for the present research.

oppression, or what it would mean to come to terms with my Irish ancestry from Counties Mayo and Clare in this dance. It would have been easier to see these things as quite distant and removed from myself. However, in the course of this project I was surprised to learn that they were not. While no ethical clearance was needed to undertake this self-inquiry, I would suggest based on my own experience that doctoral candidates employing a practice-informed and autoethnographic methodology undergo a personal ethical review that includes a remedy in the event that the work becomes too difficult or upsetting. Research should be undertaken with self-care, caution and patience regardless of background, health and ability.

Nevertheless, despite the emotional issues that arose in the course of this research, the journey and the results have been equal parts exhilarating and sobering. In the end (and along the way) the insights I have gained have been stimulating, profoundly healing and gratifying beyond my expectation, and I am excited to meet the world postdoctorally. It would be a mistake to not mention the personal calamity I brought upon myself in the course of preparing this project, whose effects set in during my second year of research leading to withdrawal from the program in the middle of my third year. I hope sharing this experience will contribute to this project being a guide for other researchers for whom dance is an intimate part of their lives and who may wish to critique it on interpersonal, mental, emotional and spiritual levels. As dance inheritances may be bound up with intergenerational trauma, with the two things often inextricably linked, there remains much for impact-driven dance researchers to explore through personal experience and critical contextual reflection.

Traumas, whether they be immediate or distant, have the capacity to break our hearts wide open. For impact-driven dancers there is nothing wrong with simply dancing our steps, whether we do so in quest of virtuosity, simply as a little exercise or in order to touch with our community. This is my suggestion to dancers who feel a little crack in the heart every time their body shakes from hitting the ground: stop trying to contain it. Let that fracture spread, follow it and keep dancing. Then, please let us know how it goes.

Introduction

Here begin the two "B" sections of the thesis. The traditions I have described henceforth inform a singular dance practice which I have characterized by the term "psychometry". The various communities and dance traditions discussed so far have contributed to my understanding of Irish step dance. In the following two chapters I explain how these traditions and communities are present in each collision within my steps and explore how the threads of my experience have shaped my personal perspective on step dance.

I begin by citing question 146 from Bishop Berkeley's early 18th-century text, *The querist: containing several queries, proposed to the consideration of the public* (Berkeley 1750). This treatise is concerned not only with philosophical debates of the time but also with how they inform and are informed by economics, style, education et al. Berkeley's question and the process of posing "queries" has inspired the theme for which I have choreographically posed psychometric questions.

In my dance, I re-step key moments from this work, using them to embody some of the human–technological encounters that inspired my movement. Using everything from gloves to corsets to dance manuals to gym workouts, each HTE took place literally before it acquired artistic manifestation. One of my key findings during this stage was that the absence of the object on stage better facilitated a creative exploration of the HTE and any potential intimate violence. At the same time it served to affirm a basic psychometrical material concept: that intimate violence lingers long after first contact. However, this absence-as-presence approach has the disadvantage of the audience failing to grasp the full choreographic meaning of the work.

I employed a personal narrative method (autoethnographic cartography meets narrative inquiry meets PTSD treatment's narrative storytelling) for each of these key development stages. This served to facilitate the meeting of self and substance in psychometric choreography. There is unfortunately little scope here to go into detail about the mechanics of developing kinetic ideas for the stage. I have never been hired to choreograph other people and I do not have an interest in doing so. Thus, I do not see this lack of documentation as a deficiency of the present study. I am often asked to write and speak however, which I welcome as my writing is inseparable from my non-theatrical life as a step dancer. I hope this approach does not devalue the languages of the body in space and time that have been developed by my choreographic forbears. Instead I hope that it will contribute to or at least support a framework for documenting and expressing the often-overlooked messy feelings that arise through dance.

In what follows I describe the production of *The Querist*. I recap of many of the final HTEs that occurred during the 25-minute solo dance show and share some of my psychometric findings (how I felt experiencing these HTEs). I encourage the reader to view the production in order to better understand these findings. Finally, I conclude by recounting an event from the post-production experience and describing what happened to me as a result of becoming *The Querist*.

Posing the Question

An Anglican bishop in a bathtub
Asks Ireland, "Whether we are not un-
Done by fashions made for other people?"
Three centuries pass, I ask what fashion
Made him own slaves and kidnap natives.

Style is never innocent. We carry
Gloves, corsets, heels and fans throughout our lives—
Hiding, showing, raising, diminishing—
Lifting towards the vogue of a lost country,
Postures of power without manuals.

Then, here comes the dancer. A system is
Changed forever by a simple gesture.

Paraphrase

The next identity I assume is that of *The Querist*, taken from Berkeley's 1725 text of the same name (Berkeley 1750). Berkeley, his immaterialist philosophy, *The Querist*'s application of rhetoric to economics and his contemporaneity with the early Irish dancing masters makes this text (and Berkeley himself) a platform from which to explore 18th-century Irish dance. In particular, this text will offer a framework for understanding how dancers expressed their encounters with style as part of their choreo-destiny and where they wished their movements to take them in life. I am not a dance theater choreographer, having learned to choreograph for dance theater strictly for the purposes of this project. The purpose of this chapter is to think with my dance academically—and to find out what is still there when I dance. My Irish step dancing before, during and after this project needs no academic framing (though it does merit some explanation). This chapter will only serve to explain how I practice Irish step dance and my research into the history of the form for the benefit of those who are interested in impact-driven dance generally. A less theatrically appealing and more academic approach does at times threaten to consume my movement, the dramaturgy and this project as a whole. This might appear to run counter to what I have outlined in my autoethnographic methodology. In my dance however, which may be considered a form of "vernacular" or "street dance", I experience a certain ambivalence, caution and skepticism, especially when it comes to theatrical re-presentations of dance forms that originate from outside the theater, such as Irish step dance, Vogue and Romani Dance. Something is lost in theatrical representation, and I feel these lived, communal dance forms do not thrive in the theater. In my experience, dance theater too often oversimplifies, exploits or erases people's experiences. It is not the artistry of the stage artist that I wish to throw into doubt, but the abilities of the spectator which I believe we as dancers tend to overestimate and engage too carelessly, particularly when attempting to communicate complex ideas and histories our audiences seldom lack the education to understand. The Anglo-Irish, colonial, slave-holding, patriarchal context of Berkeley and *The Querist* helps me stay sober and control the feelings I have developed towards the theater during a lifetime of experience as a dancer and musician. In short, Berkeley helps me to maintain an active, choreographic perspective on Critical Whiteness Studies.

My somewhat abstract use of Berkeley also helps me to better situate this work in Anglo-Irish literary discussions (of which take place within Irish-American and Irish Studies). He also helps me to keep a handle on relevant philosophical debates, furthering the reach of this project. While I certainly hope for the present work to be widely accessible, it is important to acknowledge that while HTEs and other intimate violences may be communal, in step dance they are private insofar as the dancer dances them alone. I do not mean private in the sense that they are not visible or available to observation, entertainment or manipulation, but that each dancer's dance is their own. This imposes a certain limitation. Thus, my application of Berkeley's *Querist* derives from a personal, creative decision, a kind of small dance within myself. That said, I have found that past ideas pursue us more closely than we often appreciate. For example, I currently happen to manage a software engineer who is a well-published Berkeley scholar, a fact which re-asserts the omnipresence of machines in society. Drawing on Berkeley also allows me to reach an audience of those familiar with his philosophical writings. Berkeley is a leading figure in the development of Anglophone philosophy, and his views on "immaterialism" strike a chord with my own desire to use new materialism as a method of developing self-awareness as a dancer through psychometric theory, which constitutes a kind of "material" perspective.

Berkeley is widely studied in philosophy and is tied to the development of immaterialism. Among his most famous observations is that "*esse est percipi*" or, "to be is to be perceived" (Berkeley 2003), affirming his opposition to John Locke, other materialist philosophers and scientists who asserted that objects exist independent of our perception of them. Berkeley's philosophy was doctrinal. He held the bishopric of Cloyne in Dublin, and materialism struck him as a blasphemous philosophy that dispensed with the Christian god. While Berkeley's theological biases may seem to render his views blurry, the continued failure of materialists today to prove that there is a world (or at least that the world exists as we know it be) without someone observing it keeps Berkeley and his works relevant. As discussed in the last chapter, debates around new materialism support psychometric theory and imply a more complex view of matter and its operation in the world than that presented by the early modern philosophers. While the argument for psychometric theory in dance is not so ambitious as to shed light on the nature of all things in existence, its insistence that we come to know ourselves in our contact with matter evokes a long philosophical tradition of understanding our experience of reality through our perception of things. Berkeley stands as a key figure in the development of this philosophical tradition.

In inviting Berkeley and his philosophical and economic views into my psychometric study of HTEs and the intimate violences I will be dancing, I do not aim to offer a clear position on this chicken-versus-the-egg debate or even to create my own system of intra-related agential phenomena. Instead, I will be drawing on Vogue methodology, Romani methodology and Irish step dance methodology to grapple with the fashions with which I interact in my dance. In evoking this debate and posing the question of how dance can put thought into motion, I mobilize Berkeley's philosophy so as to experience it not from just one position, but multiple—as one experience. This allows me to pursue the primary goal of psychometry, which is to not just consider how we think ourselves into being as we touch the world but simply to feel the world as it touches us. This means less claiming of space (land) and ideas (property) and more exploration of emotion and affect of contact using the language of body and soul.

Berkeley's religious thought takes a surprising turn in The Querist where rhetoric meets questions of the day-to-day in early 18th-century Ireland, as viewed from the author's privileged position. The finished work contains some 900 questions, ranging from politics to industry to the imitation of continental pleasures. While easy to dismiss as anachronistic and a lesser contribution to knowledge than his *Treatise* (Berkeley 2003), there is a practice-based methodology at work in *The Querist*. As a dancer working psychometrically, question 146 is particularly striking: "whether we are not undone by fashions made for other people?" This question is posed rhetorically, implying that Berkeley thinks the Irish are somehow being undone by the fashions of Europe. His observations are intended to reinforce the need for pastoral insight and care. I am not interested making any sort of moral statement through my dance piece, although I do think Irish traditional music and dance's close associations with regulatory bodies such as CLRG and Comhaltas Ceoltóirí Éireann[39] keeps study of the political relevant. The regulation of Irish step dancing bodies can

---

[39] An Comhaltas Ceoltóirí Éiraeann is an institution that supports Irish traditional music through local chapters, competitions.

often appear obsessive. However, a single regulatory change has the potential to alter the course of this dance community. Irish dance historian John Cullinane in his study of letters from a 1924 dance competition that took place in Dublin finds that the introduction of "light" or balletic shoes caused an uproar among attendees (Cullinane 1994: 61) as they were seen as "continental". A hundred years later, Irish step dance is often divided into "hard" and "soft" shoe categories, which for Irish step dancers a century ago would certainly have been viewed as a signal of decline. Questions of values and morality in movement are present in my own choreonavigation of the hegemonic, the marginalized and the technological, whether concerning something as simple as a shoe or as complex as AI. However, as this is an Arts Practice dance project my priority is to explore the "undoing" of my dance at the hands of "fashion." I define fashion as both that which is wearable on the human body and its intersection with style and technology. "Undoing" denotes processes of doing, making, unmaking and becoming in dance. It is framed by dualities of power including the emic/etic, hegemonic/subaltern, cosmopolitan/rural, colonial/native, queer/straight, cis/trans, et al. In summary, Berkeley's query 146 allows me to put in motion my psychometric poses both in the context of the dance work I am creating and within larger the chrono-spheres of history, futurity and the timescales of audience members.

The other benefit of engaging with Berkeley comes from his own position as a white, Christian, patriarchal Anglo-Saxon academic religious authority. We know of Berkeley because of the powerful and influential rank he had acquired at his time in history. Surely many people at this time were asking similar philosophical questions, even if their works are not preserved as well as those of this affluent, slave-holding, Indigenous-oppressing (in Ireland and North America) white Anglo-Irish clergyman. Berkeley, indeed, benefited from an apartheid system in Ireland that imposed a ten percent tithing on Catholics to the Anglican Church, did not allow them to own land and forbade the native language, Gaeilge, among other cruel prohibitions.

By assuming the identity of *the Querist* I lay claim to Berkeley's authority, white male privilege, and audacity to muse in writing of how others should think and conduct their lives. I embody this identity myself merely by being associated with Anglophone academia, as well as through my own British ancestry which has been reinforced for me through stories read to me as a child in public schools of what it means to be a citizen of the United States of America. This identity does not sit so easily beside my Irish-American and Romani identities. These contradictions they give rise to are mediated in the American context by context-switching, hybridity and racism. In posing *the Querist* I wish to ask what I can do with this identity and what it does in turn to me. What it does, among other things, is prove Berkeley's complete lack of awareness of the fact that it was in fact Anglo-Irish and British colonialism that was the undoing of Gaelic and native Irish culture, rather than influences from the European continent. There are many other such observations to be made on this question. I am unsure if my dance theater choreography conveys these realizations, but they are present within my own personal development.

Besides the positive dimension (Berkeley is a canonical authority that gets attention from other academics) and the negative dimension (Berkeley benefited from systems of oppression and should not be cited) of *The Querist*, the main reason I chose to cite this work was that I was amused by a pun: querist/queer-est. I do not think this play on words succeeds in any real way of queering the problematic figure of Bishop Berkeley, though the triviality of the pun feels subversive. Perhaps other queer and queer-aligned audience members appreciated my play on words, while others were unsure what I was getting at. Being *The Querist* meant recognizing that I was the queerest Irish dancer in the room. The queer-est pun also denotes the way I tripped over the weight of the subjects that I carried in my steps. Though colonialism and slavery are impossible burdens to carry, I have an arrogant desire to sort them out, to fix them in my project. If the grand theorizing of early modern philosophers had not come at the expense of and torture of so many, we could perhaps see it as grandiose, eccentric and amusing. Writers in the 17th and 18th centuries were very much aware of the absurdity of contemporary scholarship. Anglo-Irish satirist Jonathan Swift's first major work, published in 1694, *A Tale of a Tub* (2003) is a complex parody of religion, scholarly writing and print culture. The controversy caused by the publication of this work hindered Swift's ability to rise within the Anglican Church, as Berkeley later would. In it, he pokes fun at the frivolous, self-serving pedantry of various academic minutiae. While Berkeley's *Querist* obsesses over such minutiae as the production of linen, what women wear and the nature of various manufactured commodities, the Queer-est exists within a lineage of satire that shows some signs of self-awareness.

The Querist applies psychometric theory to a creative endeavor, posing questions informed by Anglo-Irish colonialism, print culture and the circulation of style in the Atlantic world. It is both a philosophical endeavor and a method of undertaking Arts Practice dance scholarship. Berkeley's question, "are we not undone by fashions made for other people?", refers to Irish people adopting popular continental fashion in the early 18th century. However, it can also be applied to some familiar themes of dance theater: making/un-making, global and local hybridity (Robertson 1992) and processes of dancing identity. There is also sterility present in this project. Diana Taylor's seminal text *The Archive and the Repertoire* (Taylor 2003) exposes the gap between what is captured in print/the archive and the living practice, or repertoire. Berkeley's Querist stands for dis-embodied theory (the archive), while Irish step dance and Vogue, or Step&Vogue, represent something living and embodied (the repertoire). At the meeting of these I propose a series of etudes (studies) on presentation. The etude is a western musical concept that denotes instrumental exercises intended to improve facility and teach key musical concepts (rhythm, meter, harmony, composition et al.). The etude falls somewhere between performance and private practice. An etude is more advanced than, say, playing scales, but is not supposed to be fit for concert consumption. Here, the idea of the etude captures my development process.

Development

There are many sites (and cites) of development of this work. With consideration of other axes of location (places distant but connected through my movements and presences there), I will focus on three: University College Dublin, Iveagh Fitness in Dublin and MoKS in Estonia. Like many practice-based researchers, I have needed to develop my methodology alongside my output. I consider both here.

UCD: Winter/Spring 2017

I was locked in the basement of the University College Dublin (UCD) School of English, Drama and Film. My task was simple: to dance my way out. In my fourth and final Arts Practice self-created elective module, by chance I had gained the mentorship of dance scholar, professor and dance pioneer Finola Cronin. A member of the Junk Ensemble and former member of Pina Bausch's Tanztheater Wuppertal, I had met Finola at the Dance Research Forum Ireland 2016 symposium at New York University. She recognized my fledgling status as a dance theater choreographer and generously offered to share her time, expertise and a sizable dance studio back on campus in Dublin, where I had moved that summer from Limerick. I eagerly accepted the opportunity.

I had lived in Dublin in 2008 for three months and had great success there as an artist prior to my immigration status being revoked and being deported to the United States. I had also undertaken an extended research trip there in winter 2014. On this occasion my boyfriend at the time and I watched the episode of the Saturday Night Show where Rory O'Neill AKA Panti Bliss, beloved Irish drag performer, called John Waters "homophobic". A lawsuit, the staging of Panti's Noble Call at the Abbey Theatre and a national referendum for marriage equality would follow. It seemed like in Dublin things might happen again, and so I moved back there. This would not transpire with me gaining access to the elite world of Irish dance theater nor did I find much academic or choreographical work there. Nevertheless, this is the setting of my UCD studies and later my dance training, education and rehearsal at Iveagh Fitness.

My studio solitude began in January 2017 and would continue until late April. During the semester, I gave a studio work-in-progress showing to my supervisor, Finola and some members of the local dance community at UCD and in Dublin. The studio had no windows or mirrors; the door shut absolutely. Finola would visit me a handful of times to view some of my work, provide some commentary and suggestions to take the movement further. On several occasions we met for discussion over tea in a student dining room upstairs where I was encouraged to keep doing the "real work" of making dance so that later, I would have something to write about. Other than this, I was completely alone. This experience would change how I danced forever.

At first, I clung to what was already available to me. I downloaded *Terpsichore in Sneakers* (Banes 2011) and read a few other works recommended to me by Finola. I watched dance works by Garth Fagan, Laura Dean, Joaquin Cortez, Twyla Tharp, Pina Bausch and Trisha Brown. In dance theater the only formal training I had had was on the Dunham technique of the iconic Joan Peters at Alvin-Ailey American Dance Theatre. Previously, I had helped to create new Irish Mod-Erin works with Darrah Carr Dance from 2006-2012. Having worked in musical theater I was also a (passable) chorus-dancer. More recently, my encounters with the somatic dance community in Ireland (discussed in greater detail later) taught me some further dance theater methods, albeit these were bewildering so to me as an

Irish step dancer. At the time I was not aware of anyone working with Vogue/Ballroom/House in a dance theater context. I only knew that these forms employed some references to African-American dance techniques such as "tut-ing" or re-creating poses from Egyptian iconography. Vogue has since become a more heavily trafficked artform for QTBIPOC choreographers, with curator Rashad Newsome's works having achieved global success in works such as *Assembly* at the Armory in New York City (Newsome 2023). Elsewhere on the Irish dance theater landscape I encountered the works of Jean Butler, Colin Dunne and Breandán de Gallaí. The first two of these embraced Ireland's somatic, Daghda Dance-led contemporary dance scene. The latter had developed a dance theater and storytelling technique that connected with mid-20th-century works by Patricia Mulholland who accepted Irish step dance (without deconstructing it) as an art form in its own right and who sought to celebrate its beauty theatrically. I dragged each of these and other practices and techniques into my subterranean lair, where they would then make me feel powerful for a moment, only to retreat into silliness as the room met my re-constructions with silence. As noise met silence, stillness always won, and I realized I would have to change. I was failing to dance my way out of the room.

A way forward would eventually be made by returning to my original research query. I discovered I was hunting fashion. In the early years of my graduate research, I had collected information on items of 18th-century fashion in the Atlantic world. The items I would return to constantly were gloves, high heeled shoes, wooden clogs, hats, corsets and crinolines (boned underskirts). I will describe the meaning of the items chosen for *the Querist* in the next section where I describe the production itself. For the first month I would consistently bring all these items into the studio with some hope that dancing with them would suddenly in itself become interesting. To cut the story short, it never became interesting to me in that it never seemed to truly make any sense amid the silence that had become my mentor, adjudicator and lover.[40] This can be summarized by a principle I learned in my education in Dalcroze Eurythmics, a branch of the method of music education developed by Emile Jacques-Dalcroze that involves embodied rhythmic exercises designed to teach complex musical concepts such as meter, melody and harmony. As a teacher my students would sometimes employ ideas that were somewhat para-ambulatory, such as the bouncing of balls to the beat of the music. My own teachers had always balked at such proposals for it would mean the ball experiencing the beat in itself, not the bouncer of the ball. However, in Eurythmics, the ball is not our assistant, but is instead an actor unto itself. The emphasis is transferred from moving musician to moving object. This principle runs counter to the psychometric principle that it is the object that is in the process of becoming, not the dancer in conjunction with the object. Similarly, in my dance, it was the glove, corset or crinoline that would be brought into the present to become the focus of movement, play and reflection. These objects also have a familiar, steampunk-ish quality that opens the work to overtones of drag performance, burlesque and circus performance art. The psychometric exercises that had felt so meaningful at the Blue Teapot descended into a predictable kind of over-the-top puppetry. This in itself was potentially interesting, but seemed to supplant the experiences within and for the body in space and time that I was undergoing at this time in the context of dance theater and contemporary dance.

I had dragged a camera to my lair, and found this also to be problematic. In my 20s in New York City I had created my own improvisatory movement style as an Irish step dancer and harper. A regular patron at a gay bar I was working at advised me to just let the camera roll. He said this is what Twyla Tharp had done back in her day. The idea was to let the camera capture whatever came out of my body, watch it and set about composing movement from the best bits. Seeing as the patron who had

---

40 I mean in the sense that I was pursuing something pleasurable to my "libidinal" choreographer-researcher impulses.

recommended doing this had watched Tharp rise to prominence in the 60s and 70s, this advice felt like a way forward. In the studio however, there was another artwork that kept coming back to haunt me; namely one of Yoko Ono's sky pieces, *Sky TV* (1966). I had seen this work performed in Cleveland during my college days (Cleveland Museum of Art 2002), and was struck by the audaciousness of the piece which consisted simply of filming the sky and playing the footage on a TV monitor in an art gallery. The viewer reflecting on the piece would be struck by sensation that they were being watched, in ever increasing measure and by novel means.

Elise Morrison argues that:

> Staging works on street corners and online websites, in political protests and academic conferences, as well as in more traditional spaces of theatrical performance and installation art enables surveillance artists to present in distilled form pressing techno-cultural quandaries and ethical questions of the digital information age. (Morrison 2015: 126)

Surveillant art gives audiences an opportunity to consider the ethical dilemmas and perilous futurity involved in being watched. Surveillance has been around for far, far longer than modern surveillance technology. The Ordinance Survey, begun by the British in 1820, was to date the largest mapping project ever carried out and was undertaken to support further exploitation of natural resources in Ireland. The practice of cadastral mapping[41] has been a vital tool of colonialism since at least Roman times. It weaponizes cartography and print as means of supplanting and re-writing local knowledge, practice and lives. Brian Friel's play *Translations* explores the disparities between English and Irish communities during the time when the Ordinance Survey was carried out shortly before the An Gorta Mór / the Irish Potato Famine (Friel 2005). As dance manuals were also an important

---

41 Mapping for resources versus mapping for cultural meaning, such as with indigenous cartography;

tool for disseminating colonial ideals through "orchesography",[42] we can conclude that Irish dancers have been choreonavigating surveillance for a long time. The methods we use to remember dance have a direct bearing on technology used for surveilling colonized subjects and transforming them into capitalized objects. For this reason, I am wary of the presence of the video camera in the rehearsal studio.

As I examined my own connection to the Judson Dance Movement, the apparent randomness of movement in some of the choreographer's work gives me pause. I watched a video recording of Yvonne Rainer's genre-defining work, "Trio-A" and was struck by the apparently arbitrary nature of the movements, which reminded me of Ono's clouds moving across the TV in *Sky TV*. Irish step dance practice is rich with mnemonics that are designed to help dancers memorize their dance. Romani dance forms, similarly, are rich with vocalizations based on the Romani language that help dancers to think through and communicate steps with other dancers and to pass embodied knowledge between generations. Despite the pedagogical erasure of gadje Flamenco dancers, these vocalizations (*letras*) are central to the history of the form (Ríos-Terheun 2018). The presence of a camera threatens to undo all of this as the agency of human experience gives way to the "banality" of a recording camera that will almost inevitably be used for "evil" (Arendt and Elon 2006). The trawling of the internet videos for the purpose of training Artificial Intelligence adds an unspeakable layer of horror to this. Video cameras as *the* method of documentation of the body can have the effect of rendering creative works, data and the gestures of human life meaningless—and devoured. I offer this interpretation of *Trio-A* not as a critique of Rainer's intent. I have no idea if she actually used video to create this work (although that is how I first viewed the piece). Nevertheless, it was clear to me that Tharp's style was made possible by surveillance and

---

42 Orchesography literally translates to "writing" or "drawing" of dance. It was first used by Thoinot Arbeau in 1588 and re-used by Raoul-Auger Feuillet in the development of his dance notation (Foley 2013).

that it presented an intimate violence through a form of video surveillance that dancers still feel in their bodies today.

I realize now that in refusing to embrace the video recording of improvised movement I was searching for my own orchesography, one informed by the direct fashioning of objects. To return to the principle of An Draoí: the Druids were said to have been literate, though they chose not to write many of their teachings given how dangerous those teachings could be should they fall into the wrong hands. While we may not be able to know for sure whether this was indeed the case, I recognize this impulse in Irish dance. In class with my Irish dancing masters, Donny Golden and Tessie Burke, I do not recall ever writing anything down. Some knowledge is best experienced directly and passed on communally. This applies to Romani and Vogue/Ballroom/House. In my budding dance theater choreography, if I cannot carry it with or inside me, I do not carry it. In so doing I value oral, in-person and embodied means of transmission above the written and audio or visual recorded.

As the semester wore on, I would leave these pieces of fashion and surveillance in my dance bag. Nevertheless, I realized that they still clung to my body. My initial psychometric tasks had an ontology of their own that endured with or without the object. As regards to notation, I would use my memory combined with some manual note taking to be sure that I captured what those steps were. This served more as a memory exercise than as notes to be consulted for analysis later. Mind-mapping was also useful for connecting thoughts and ideas that were floating in my mind. As I kept searching for a compositional method that worked for me and as I tried to move in the studio I came up against a new problem: the problem of hands.

On the Silencing of Shoes

Before I introduce the turning point in the development of *the Querist* that came through the hands, I would like to address the silencing and absence of footwear in this piece. As my project developed and was disseminated among the broader Irish step dance community, I was confronted with the difficult decision of whether to silence my shoes, that is, to leave them off entirely during this performance. The decision not to wear shoes was a decision to take as an Irish step dancer, and it was dictated in part owing to lack of access to dance spaces where I could wear the shoes necessary to execute a hard shoe reel, hornpipe or jig. I did explore dancing in my sneakers, or in rubber-soled shoes. However, this idea ended up informing another work during the lead-up to the performance of *The Querist*.

Through 2014-2015 I began to explore dancing in rubber shoes. Rubber-soled shoes are the de facto shoe of Irish step dancers for a number of decades as they are the shoes worn to mark our steps during a rehearsal, when we are practicing a difficult combination, while waiting in line and in the course of our day-to-day life, which thereby is transformed into a kind step dance of its own. Rubber shoes proliferated in the late 19th to early 20th centuries. During the 20th century, they came to transform the way that people danced. Rubber softens complicated surfaces and silences impact. As rubber replaced the vertically-inclined leather and wooden-soled shoe, impact was transformed from sound potential into kinetic potential, opening up a multi-directional field of play. This led to the introduction of a number of barefoot dance techniques to popular dance forms. It effectively spelled an end to centuries of sound-producing percussive dance, forcing it into commercial and nationalistic arenas.

I became fascinated by the idea of rubber-soled impact-driven dance. My 2015 work *When the Rubber Meets the Dirt Road* explores the meeting of time, disembodied sound, the sensation of waiting for the past to become the future and the primal quality of a dirt road by means of the rubber shoe (Russell Patrick Brown

2015). The dance lives somewhere in between all these things. Since this dance was published on YouTube, I had planned for rubber shoes to be the center of my doctoral project. Then, in 2017, I abandoned this plan since by then the wearing of rubber shoes had become widespread within the Irish dance community, beginning with Colin Dunne who wore them in his production, *Concert*. In 2016 I remarked to Colin that it did not make sense to mic a metal-tipped Irish dance hard shoe in the way he was doing; the shoe is already amplified. The choreographic interest might instead come from mic'ing a shoe that you could not hear, such as I was doing with rubber shoes. Colin took this idea on board and implemented it brilliantly, drawing on his years of experience experimenting with the sounds of Irish step dance. The *Irish Times* noted that Colin's sneaker-clad performance showed, "how every dance comes from the simple act of stepping" (Michael Seaver 2017), which to me proves the value of calceological[43] dance research. Dance artists such as Sibeál Devitt would later follow suit. Given the growing popularity of the rubber shoe, I did not see this as a channel worth exploring further in a theatrical arena. Going forward, as in the case of my other clothes, I found the absence of the shoe more interesting and indeed more suitable to my budget.

Asking in Motion

Halfway through my residency at UCD, I had an epiphany. After weeks of imitation (and desperation), my body did something that felt as if it emerged from silence: I had discovered a question. With my carefully selected development music switched off (Finola had encouraged a limited use of music from the beginning), I stood facing the area of the room where I imagined the audience would sit. I felt naked, but my bareness had the brutality to meet the silence of the room, and still be there after the collision. My arms

---

43 Calceology refers to the study of footwear.

were hanging at my side when suddenly my right hand assumed a right angle to my body. As this happened my left foot pushed down turning my body to the right while I looked brusquely in the direction of where my right hand was leading my body. This felt daring, and I quickly resumed standing still with my arms at my sides. I repeated this twist and flex a few times, each time feeling like I was asking something of my hand, which was active in my mind owing to the gloves that I had worn. The third time I assumed the pose my left hand decided to join the interrogation, placing itself a few inches higher than my right hand. Next, my right hand jumped and stacked a few inches higher than my left, and so on until my flexed hands were trying desperately to go higher but could not because they had hit the limit of my height and reach.

I was awake. Suddenly the earlier compositional styles became available to me. They offered methods of developing an idea, of questioning further. Choreography became a way of answering a question and asking more questions, across the floor, through the air, on the ground, with passion and with defeat. I would call this piece "The Glove", and it survived into *The Querist*. As an Irish dancer I had solved the problem of what to do with my hands, namely by opening myself to asking through space and time. This orchesography of embodied questioning in a haunted space (a theater) informs the present research.

Iveagh Fitness: 2016/2017

Despite their seeming absence from department stores, fashion magazines and online shopping websites, corsets remain extremely popular. Women wear them, but they are much more popular among men, particularly on Instagram, YouTube and TikTok. It is an extreme look, and for many represents an unattainable aesthetic of physical beauty that emphasizes narrow waists and flat stomachs that accentuates the buttocks, male genitalia, breasts and shoulders. The name "corset", however, has fallen out of favor outside fetish communities. Today we call them "abs".

From the time I began step dancing again at the age of 22 in Manhattan, I have practiced, rehearsed and developed new steps in group exercise studios in gyms and fitness clubs. Pubs, nightclubs, train platforms, parks and piers were also vital spaces to helping me develop my own dance vernacular and to supporting my physical training. However, it was necessary on occasion to rent dance studio space. On occasions when the cost of renting a studio was prohibitive, I used fitness studios that were "free" to use since I was already paying the membership fee to do my acrobatic weight training. In these spaces the mirrors and semi-sprung floors were safe for dancing, and they were typically almost completely empty during the day and late at night. Whenever I needed to hone the finer points of my technique or run choreography full out, fitness studios were essential. Fitness studios allured me for another reason; gym workouts long ago became the new ballet.

As Linda Tomko observes, during the 19th and 20th centuries in America, physical fitness became essential to "fit"-ing into an ever urban, industrial society (Tomko 1999). The value and aesthetics of fitness were mediated by universities, social reformers and public health officials. Dance was also used to pursue the same goals. 20th-century marketing celebrated idealized bodies, further spreading these aesthetics. Fitness thereby came to occupy the role that balletic training had in earlier courtly, aristocratic society. The wealthy have embraced gym culture with elite health clubs such as Equinox and Lifetime targeting the 1% and the aspirational 99%, I have always been fascinated with the aspects of Irish step dance that connect not only to ballet but also to the postmodern world of weightlifting, cross-functional fitness routines, personal trainers and fitness influencers. In Irish contexts similar values have taken root. When I first moved to Ireland in 2008 there was one gym that echoed the glamorous gyms of New York City, the resplendent

Crunch Gym in Temple Bar, Dublin. In the two decades since, gym culture has exploded and come to live alongside earlier physical training methods including those advanced by the Gaelic Athletic Association and Irish step dancing. All of this is merely to say that I enjoy practicing my steps, my acrobatics and my weight training at the gym—much to the dismay of the ever-more hyper-masculine society we are living in—and that I am using my academic research to justify doing this.

Iveagh Fitness Club is located in Dublin 8, on the south side of the River Liffey between Christchurch Cathedral and St Patrick's Cathedral. Its entrance is on a side street off of the thoroughfare that is Dame Street. The Iveagh buildings are grade-listed (historic and protected) and form part of the Iveagh Trust, an organization dating to the early 20th century founded to promote public housing and health for Dubliners. The Iveagh gym was opened in the old Iveagh Trust Public Baths, connecting it to the history of changing social and health values within Ireland. These facts are incidental to the present research. Above all, the gym was affordable, near enough to where I lived in Smithfield and it had the weight lifting and acrobatic equipment I needed to carry out my training. It also had a marvelous almost-always-empty group fitness studio with wooden floors. Throughout the winter of 2016/2017 until the performance of *The Querist*, Iveagh Fitness was where I created and rehearsed the majority of my choreography.

Throughout my time at Iveagh my training consisted of five parts: weight training, acrobatic training, Fleming Elastxx,[44] Step&Vogue and, of course, practicing *The Querist*. The weight training helped with my hereditary propensity for obesity by raising my resting metabolism, and the acrobatic training (handstands and inversion work hanging from a bar) provided a creative outlet for me as my step dancing increasingly had by now become a focus of work and research. I had originally thought I would include some of these acrobatic moves and gestures in my

---

44 More in the next chapter, AngelAI.

productions, but in both cases I opted to exclude these moves owing to time and production constraints.

Step&Vogue was a thrilling, challenging medium for me, all the more so as I was unsure what I would ever do with it. Being a white-passing cisgender male brought a measure of anxiety around what I was doing with Vogue and what I wanted from it. Given the long and ongoing history of appropriation, this is understandable. This had not been a concern for me, at least as far as I could see, in New York City. I was not a Ball walker and was not trying to be, nor was I trying to practice Vogue in a commercial arena, which did not exist at that time as it does now. Vogue for me and Celso was a means of sharing community and exchanging cultural knowledge. Celso invited me to welcome Irish-ness and Romanipen into my dance, and so I did. This resulted in developing new forms of Vogue and Irish step dance and articulating a shared understanding between these forms (each with their own eclectic histories as competitive, battling dance forms) that continues to inform my life and my movement.

In Ireland, the future of Vogue was unclear. Many colleagues encouraged me to teach it more widely. I taught one Vogue workshop at Iveagh Fitness as an experiment, which was well-attended by Irish non-nationals only. A week later at the YMCA nearby a prominent Dublin drag queen set up her own Vogue dance classes. While she did not have experience in Vogue/Ballroom/House, she had much more support from Irish people than me and so I never repeated my own class. I had considered starting a House, but I had not succeeded at making friends in Dublin, so this was a non-starter. I did, however, get to perform Step&Vogue at The George, Ireland's most famous gay bar. It was an honor to receive an invitation from the drag queens who ruled there, but when you are not in drag and you are a dancing man on stage at a gay bar, the expectation is that you are a stripper or a go-go boy. I was opposed to this as my uncle had been a famous gay stripper, and I was not interested in continuing the family business. Ultimately Galway continued to welcome my Vogue dancing in addition to my work at The Blue Teapot, and I taught very well-attended workshops by Irish and non-Irish nationals alike for Genevieve Ryan Dance Academy and Galway Dance Project. My experience sharing Vogue had seemed to run its course, and that was that. This did not greatly bother me as most students simply wanted a combination to take home, they were typically not looking to adopt a new lifestyle, which is what Vogue represents to me.

Returning to *The Querist*, while at UCD I developed a methodology to allow me to pose my dance research, and at Iveagh I learned to hone who I was as the querier. I was creating my choreo-destiny, my hope that in my body, my movement and my expression I would become who I wished to be in the world. This was the hope that, by drawing on both the good and the bad, I could craft my own freedom. To me I could not with confidence present The Querist without first having lived the dance I was presenting. With this armory of embodied life in place and questions at hand, in August 2017 I headed to Estonia.

MoKS: August 2017

From the beginning of my PhD journey, I developed a close friend and colleague in a classmate, Maria Kerin. Maria is an artist, dancer/choreographer and curator based in Ennistymon, County Clare. Growing up in the scenic Burren of North Clare, Maria's practice explores the intersections of the local and global, ecology and somatic practice. She combined a choreographical rigor with an open mind to people from all over the world that continues to inspire me. Perhaps what I found most moving was her patience with my own skepticism with somatic contemporary dance's ideals, and her invitation to just feel myself. It is impossible to summarize another's artistic life, but I can say with confidence that Maria has an incredible gift for facilitation. Many times by her fire alongside her husband Michael I came to know my way around my mind and who I was becoming. In this way, the work emerged from me.

In the summer of 2017 I was nearing my first major Arts Practice work production date in September, and Maria and Michael invited me to join them for a week in Estonia to further develop my work and join in a meeting of artists they were hosting. In August I flew into Tallinn and took a bus to Tartu, where Maria and Michael picked me up and showed me around. Michael was Irish and had been living and working in Estonia since the 1980s. He had an encyclopedic knowledge of Estonian culture, history and language. I felt very much the uncultured American, so this trip was already entirely thrilling to me. As I traveled around Estonia, the legacies of colonialism and slavery under Russian, German, Danish and Swedish regimes had to be frequently explained to me so that I could better understand the Estonian people and their history. As I traveled around Estonia and saw abandoned factories and buildings from the "big days" of the USSR I oddly felt myself transported back to Cleveland, Ohio. Throughout the 19th century until the late 20th century, Cleveland was an industrial steel center that was left to rust from the 1970s when manufacturing moved overseas. While Estonian culture and government, bolstered by the European Union, remains strong, the ruins of the Cold War linger, bringing me back to a childhood of nuclear bomb drills, military pageantry and the paradoxes of nationalism.[45]

We headed southeast to the town of Mooste, about twenty miles from the Russian border to a now-closed artist studio called MoKS run by artists Evelyn and John Grzinich. On the grounds of an old 19th-century colonial Bavarian manor house, with Maria's encouragement I learned to let go of all my research and my dance training and to once again allow something new to emerge.

---

45 Some nationalist paradoxes: nationalism is as much about unification as it is about separation from the "other"; nationalist revolutions supplanted previous oppressive economic paradigms only to create their own; and also that freedom for some can mean slavery and oppression for others.

My rehearsals took place daily in the old Soviet Culture House. The light was perfect, the wooden floors pleasant to the touch and the odd company I kept was eerily resistant to my overly friendly American sensibilities. I was armed with my fabulous sense of myself as a Step&Voguer armed with psychometric questions—and it all felt ridiculous. I do not mean that the movement or my feeling of myself felt ridiculous, but that something essential was absent.

Maria, Michael and the resident artist community continued to share their many decades of experience with me. Debates and lively discussions on the grounds, over home-cooked meals and with other artists-in-residence kept my mind moving. At this point in my Arts Practice research I was absolutely sophomoric; no matter the subject of the conversation I thought I had an answer, and when I did not have an answer I threw out a tangent. All the while Maria continued to embody her somatic practice: ever-present, absolute and complete as oxygen. As a know-it-all, this was unbearable to me and only drove me further to retreat into thought. Then by grace, there was a crack.

Maria had known for some time of my shoe fetish and my need to dig deeper than the mic'ing of rubber shoes. She suggested I speak to John, an American composer, husband to Evelyn and father to their child. He was a sound artist as well. I entered his work studio and rambled on for some time about my research. Then he asked me, "What about the floor?" John suggested I consider whether it was the shoe or the floor making the noise—why not let the floor make the noise instead of the shoes, perhaps by dancing on sheet paper and ripping it. He described multiple tactile-sonic approaches that I could use. They were all so clever, simple and obvious. Here I had been speaking for so long about not taking shoes for granted that I had forgotten how much I needed the ground as well. I went to bed.

I woke up early, went outside, and went for a walk. I had taken to meandering around the grounds of the former estate, enjoying the history, nature and the opportunity to play in my movement. This early morning pink of the sun seemed to touch the world a bit more gently than normal and the air was just a breath lighter. Even in the summer the weather was cold, but today a kiss of summer mist rose from the ground. Next to a barn turned wedding venue I stopped, staring blankly not into where an audience would be, but into rolling hills and farmland which brought me back to my childhood in Ohio. Somewhere between Maria's somatic invitation, John's passing floor comments and the weight of the historical research I was carrying out, I felt the ground underneath me fall away. The disappearance of the grass underneath me was as unexpected as it was slow. As the earth underneath me drifted, I found I was leaning. My arms remained at my side and my legs aligned with my spine. However, my feet refused to let go of the falling dirt beneath me. My eyes saw the world tilt. My ankles were straining from the flexion that was all that stood between me and falling. In this nowhere I put on my high heels; I rose to the balls of my feet: leaning, tilting, swaying. The corset held in my breath. My crinoline swung in circles as I continued to lean on top of a world that kept shifting.

With tears running down my face, I had found an answer to the questions I was posing. My world was undone by fashion, and I felt it. If I truly believed there was a multi-temporal psychometric relationship between the body and technology and that this relationship lived on in dance, then it will be present when I dance. This revelation was not too different from the one I had experienced at UCD. At UCD I had discovered an embodied open mind that asked a question. This time, I found an open heart that answered this question. Our care for the past, our lives in the present and our hopes for the future shape all forms of materialism, and our love can carry everything.

Production

The program of *"The Querist", Or, Questions Posed By A Contemporary "Travelling Dance Master"*, staged September 20, 2017 at the Irish World Academy of Music and Dance in Theater Two of the University of Limerick in the Mid-West of Ireland, reads as follows:

A 'querist' is one who asks questions or inquires. As an Irish step dancer, investigating flicks, hops and cuts is what I do. Through silent and sonic relationships to the souls of my feet, I stamp and leap and move across the floor, finding new ways to twist in upon myself.

An Arts Practice academic inquiry presents the opportunity to keep this self-delectative process in the center of my Irish traditional dance doctoral research. But the floor has changed. Scholarship from around the world opens the ground to a dark colonial past. My lead-around must now reach past farmers in their fields to the wild stillness of Flaggy Shore, to the marble halls of France and Italy and to the wide ocean, returning to Ireland through feet of all colors.

Almost three hundred years after it was written, Bishop Berkeley's *The Querist* still raises interesting questions at an economic, political, religious, philosophical and sartorial crossroads in Ireland. When I read this unusual text at the beginning of my master's degree, it marked the unraveling of my dancing while also helping me define this cosmic floor I find myself upon. The most salient question, 146, asks: **'Whether we are not undone by fashions made for other people?'**

There is talk of the 'new Ireland', a post-Marriage Equality Referendum Ireland. In the halls of Berkeley's Alma Mater, queer theory and postcolonial discourse shakes hegemonic foundations. Foreign fashions infect a generation of new dancers and athletes looking beyond the pale of a nationalized dancing and sporting body. As a Step, Vogue and contemporary dancer, I feel lost.

In The Querist, or, Questions Posed by a Contemporary

Travelling Dance Master, I 'pose' question 146. The act of posing through fashion, gesture and gender comes from New York LGBTQI+ African-American and Latino Vogue Ball culture, and was given to me on Christopher Street Pier while I was practicing my jigs and reels by members of the Royal House of LaBeija. The 'quare'ness of the whole thing is *The Querist*, yet also personal.

I have curated a constellation of questions that have emerged from a year of studio study. I have explored 146 on the floors of Irish dance clubs, universities, train stations, fitness clubs, circus centers, art studios and both rural and urban kitchen floors. I have encountered old and new Ireland. The people I have met there—seen and unseen—guide my query. Tonight I begin to share my findings. I ask and answer in step and in vogue.

Music: 'Carolan's Welcome', 'Carolan's Receipt for Drinking', 'Eleanor Plunkett'; Composed by Turlough Carolan; Played by Patrick Ball on Wire Strung Harp (1983, 1985)

Lighting and Sound Design: Róisín Berg

Costume: Unitard, Copelia Ballet; Blue Top, Lululemon Yoga

I, **Russell Patrick Brown**, am a dancer, choreographer and educator based in Dublin. In New York City I studied Irish step dance with Donny Golden and Vogue with Celso Satori LaBeija. Maria Kerin, Dr. Finola Cronin and Maureen Fleming have been influences in contemporary dance. I received my BA in Music from Baldwin-Wallace University Conservatory and my MA in Irish and Irish-American Studies from New York University.

Some of the HTEs in the production are as follows. First, I will provide some historical facts about the fashions that I use and my embodied narrative premise for engaging the HTE before identifying some psychometric fictions about them. By fiction I refer not to lies, but to the story that is created in feeling:

Travelling Dancing Master

(Fact) During the early modern era into the late modern, dancing masters disseminated style throughout the Atlantic world, often travelling to do so.

(Premise) As a Step&Vogue dancer travelling in Ireland and teaching the form on a few occasions, I felt I was moving in the footsteps of earlier dancing masters—repeating undoing and becoming at the hands of fashion.

(Fiction) I feel the intimate violence of the Irish dancing master mapping their own understanding of the Irish landscape in the face of the Ordinance Survey, often alongside Hedge school teachers who offered education to Catholics who were forbidden to receive education. Irish step dance is an Indigenous countermap to colonial cadastral maps. I feel the complications of the term "master" and its implied relationship with "slave". In "travelling" I feel the erasure of Roma and Traveller dancers who travelled and taught, often interacting and exchanging with others on the road and on the seas.

Itinerant Harpers

(Fact) Under the reign of Queen Elizabeth I, during the Plantation of Ulster and through the subsequent Flight of the Earls from Ireland *na filidh* (the aristocratic poetic class of Ireland), whose works were performed by a *racaire* (reciter of poems) and accompanied by a *cruitnoir* (harper) were decimated (Rimmer 1977). With their patronage gone, these three roles were combined into one, were generally referred to as Itinerant harpers by the Ango-Irish ascendancy and their roles endured for roughly for a century and a half.

Toirdhealbhach Ó Cearbhalláin (Turlough Carolan) is the most famous of these harpers, and his works are the most enduring in the Irish tradition.

(Premise) Carolan's liminal status, contemporaneity with travelling dancing masters and the beauty of his works, mixing Renaissance and Gaelic traditions alike, are the reasons I have chosen his music to accompany my dance.

(Fiction) Carolan's performances for Protestant "big houses" and his planxties (dedications) for the people in them guided me to the channels of power dynamics continually at play in music and dance. Who is paid? What does it mean to get paid as a performer? Carolan's blindness which led him to harping helps me see the gifts of my own disabilities. The loss of the harper tradition for roughly a century does not hurt as much as meeting scholars who call those of us who feel connected to it as frauds. An Comhaltas's advice to adjudicators to decide if they will consider Carolan's music as "Irish" makes my dance feel risky, dismissible (Notes for Adjudicators. Prepared by Comhaltas Ceoltóirí Éireann as a Guide to Those Adjudicating Competitions for Irish Traditional Music and Singing at Fleadhanna Cheoil and Other CCE Functions 1987).

Dancing Manuals

(Fact) Dancing manuals were one of the many kinds of books to emerge during the rise of print in the early modern era. They included instruction on how to do the most popular dances of the age, and often were notated with orchesography. They enabled appropriation and the dis-embodiment of dance, and enabled style in the form of gesture, posture and motion and circulate widely across the globe. Due to its dictations on fashion, *The Querist* acts as a kind of dance manual.

(Premise) I styled the cover of the program as one of these verbose dancing manuals. My dancing with intimate violence becomes my orchesography and my pedagogy. I built embodied etudes around these cites/sites.

(Fiction) The challenges, excitement and intrigue of

consuming motion through text fills me with power and the potential to re-make the world in my image. My failure to put into documentation my experience in turn humbles me. My desire to map movement in print feels colonial, my desire to hold the map in myself feels much more honest. Dancing manuals remind me of social media platforms. TikTok and Instagram's opt-in surveillance (in most cases we are choosing to be observed) of moving bodies and the "viral" replication of them presses questions on the cartography of choreography. What is moral and ethical? What is actually copied in these processes?

Études (Studies)

(Fact) Western classical education in schools, conservatories and universities include methods to develop "technique", or exercises for the refinement of movement patterns designed to help musicians and dancers alike regularly and consistently produce the same results. Many of these, such as the five positions of ballet, have been developed over centuries of development of a white, colonial, aristocratic ideal of how bodies should look, move and sound. In the 20th century, these ideals have been subsumed by consumerism's adoption of the "fit" body that exercises to fit in.

(Premise) Given the axis of study involved in my dance, it was more authentic for me to build a show around the idea of studies in dance, or in the case of *The Querist* studies on the posing of questions as they relate to human–technological encounters. This gave me many problems with which I could explore through posing questions and answers.

(Fiction) I am inspired to explore the capabilities of technique and its expressive, representative and creative limits. Studies protected me from having to truly explore who I am in motion; I have drills and patterns to protect me and the better I execute them, the more capital I have on stage as a dancer. In creating technical exercises for Step&Vogue I could more carefully consider meeting points of these two dance forms. In posing fashion as I understand it, intent feels arbitrary yet inevitably moving towards consumer/consumed. This point has been made countless times before me, however. I surrender to this and get on with making my performance "good". Good in Irish step and Vogue, however can be developed in drills but is demonstrated in dance battles and the triumph of one dancer over another.

Fashion

(Fact) A great deal can be said about what we wear and how we have come to wear it. Starting from the ground up, bare feet have come to represent abject poverty (Riello 2006: 20), unless you are wealthy then it can be referred to as "grounding" and "freedom". Historically, wooden shoes were associated with hard labor, including through slavery (Ibid.: 14). Leather-soled shoes were for the more affluent, although the quality of wooden or leather shoes helped distinguish class. Consumerism and production of trees and cowhide also played a role in which type of footwear was worn where (Ibid.: 34). In the Irish case leather would have been worn by working classes only on Sundays for church—and for dancing. The high heel was originally worn by men, and would later become associated with ladies footwear. More study of this topography as it can be applied to our understanding of dance is needed.

Moving up to the legs and torso, I cite crinolines and corsets. Often called whale-bone skirts as they were made out of the bones of whales, crinolines were part of a family of fashions intended to primarily alter the shape of women, specifically by providing a structured petticoat that could extend the skirt out to the sides as in the case of panniers, in the back with a bustle or in round shape in the case of crinolines. Many women died through immolation wearing these fashions. These complex garments could easily catch fire, particularly as floor lanterns were common and it was not possible to easily get out of the many layers of petticoats and the crinoline itself, thus the women were burned alive. Structured petticoats were typically accompanied by the wearing of corsets, or a supportive undergarment designed to narrow the waist and accentuate buttocks, hips and shoulders.

Extending out in the arms and hands, gloves and hand fans and hand fans were quintessential pieces of colonial fashions. I carried out little research into the history of these objects but I recognize their significance.

Lastly, the fashions related to standing and sitting felt relevant to my dancing, in particular the evolution of flooring and chairs. While I am not aware of any comprehensive studies on the usages of dirt versus wood versus stone flooring or the prevalence of chairs in household decor, in my research I began to notice patterns. In terms of floors, earthen floors were considered for the poor, while wood and stone floors were used in increasing popularity. Likewise, I have found no references to wealthy people in the early modern period squatting on the ground; if they are at rest they are lounging on a couch or sitting in a chair. Meanwhile, for rural, working and enslaved classes of people there is ample evidence of squatting on the ground, including upon earthen floors.

(Premise) For my feet, I decided to wear no shoes. I represent the question of shoes by wearing a leotard that goes down the ankle, exposing the bare skin of my feet where shoes could be. I often dance onto the balls of my feet, affirming the presence of high heel aesthetics long after contact.

For the corset and the crinoline, my weight loss and muscular build seemed to accomplish the goals of these manipulative garments.

Like the problem of wearing shoes, I wore a long-sleeved shirt so that my hands may be exposed, functioning to draw attention to the hands in the opposite manner in which gloves and hand fans do the same. Darkening the scrim upstage added to this effect for the hands and feet.

In one section I begin in a squat on the ground, and while slowly walking down stage right I gradually ascend to standing upon the balls of feet.

(Fiction) Through technique, the muscles of my feet feel exposed, mechanical and industrious. I am aware of how heavy clogs make walking on the balls of the feet impossible, and similarly impact what dance moves are possible to execute with the feet. Bare feet on well-manicured dance flooring feels like a contradiction of power, a dance with authenticity. It feels like I have come full circle by being barefoot and letting whatever is held in my feet from the histories of clogs and leather shoes to show themselves in dance.

"Look at my shoe" to me is the history of pointing our toes in dance. I imagine many experts in Renaissance dance would disagree with me on that, however for women in particular the feet are hidden under the layers of petticoats, so pointing the foot is necessary if you want anyone to ever see what your feet are doing. I say why not, why not have a look at my shoe while my imaginary petticoats swing around the stage? The edges of movement between bare feet, wooden shoes and leather shoes mix, my dance navigates between them and their various usages in different societies which shaped the formation of percussive dance as we know it today.

For gloves and fans, my hands are reshaped in the image of them. I am wearing gloves, holding a fan and wearing jewelry, and I am showing them off, I am showing me off. I sometimes splay my hands into a fan shape to explore these gestures further.

From the grounded-ness of squatting to standing on the balls of my feet, I feel the precarity of those who dared to move in such a way, and how high so many had to climb (if they could at all) and how very far one could fall in the colonial world that birthed ballet.

There are other HTEs present within this work, and they are too numerous to mention. This is also by no means an exhaustive list of all that I have thought, felt and experienced in this dance. I encourage the reader to watch the 25-minute production so that they may feel more.

Aftermath

Much to my surprise, when I jumped in the air and landed in a split, nothing broke. What little of my costume I was still wearing after doing a striptease held together. The stage did not fall apart from my sudden crashing weight and my body felt perfectly limber and free of pain. At this point, the late-teen, early twenty-something audience screamed and started banging on the stage. It was exhilarating to play as this character, to express myself in the familiar New York Downtown nightclub/performance art style, to share my Old and New Way Vogue and to perform Irish step dancing to a dance beat. To mix Vogue with Irish step dance felt natural in my body, and it seemed to be received as if these things belonged together. My greatest pride came from the fact that my hot pants stayed up and did not slide down my waist because I had finally lost the weight to fit comfortably in them.

It was the night of Club GASS, a LGBTQIA+ dance party put together by a few community leaders on the Galway nightlife scene. Club GASS was held monthly at the Róisín Dubh in the City Center, a few doors down from the Blue Teapot. I was referred to Martin and Kiki, the producers of the event, by some friends who knew I was interested in performing on the nightlife scene. It was two months after my performance of *The Querist* in Limerick, and Martin had put me up in one of his co-producer's holiday rental apartments nearby. We hung out for the day, sharing drinks and hot toasties at a pub on a chilled November afternoon. We spoke about the day-to-day of queer life in Ireland. I had rarely felt so at home.

I had prepared two numbers for that night. The first I called *ManWithAFan*. The title was a play on the alliterative "Man With a Van" advertisements that I had seen around Dublin, and I had used this company during my move to the city. The performance began with an open hand fan on top of my head. The fan had extra silk fabric which hung down covering my face. I wore several heavy necklaces and see-through mesh baggy pants. I started off performing some slow gestures and poses to my own music—a slow triplet-pattern harpsichord tune in a minor key. When this piece was over, the beat dropped, and I let it rip as a dancer. My second number was more playful and involved a top hat, a long, sleeveless opera coat and my Irish dance ghillies. My gloves, hat and jacket came off during the course of a light striptease as I strutted about, mixing in Step&Vogue. I hated dancing shirtless as, contrary to the stereotypical view of Romani dancing, we do not like to bare our skin during our dances.

After an evening of Irish drag acts and Euro pop dance music, we posed for a picture outside on the canal. My jacket definitely got soaked as I crouched down so that the queens would not have to, and I could not have been happier.

It was the end of fall term 2017 and back home at Smithfield my year lease with The Richmond apartments was up for renewal. It was time to decide what was best for my finances, for my research and for myself. As I crunched the numbers it was clear to me that I was running at a financial loss, and life in Dublin had become unfeasibly expensive. After the weekend I had just had in Galway, it was clear I had chosen the wrong city. For the last year I had been drawn to being a web developer, app developer and software engineer. I had built the latest Dance Research Forum Ireland website in 2016, and in 2017 I had built my own website to advertise my dancing and dance instruction. At this time the startup world was booming, and I felt left out of current scientific and technological innovation. Besides all this, I had a terrible feeling that something very bad was coming, and I needed to get back to the USA and become financially stable in whatever way I could. A little over two years later, Ireland would lock down for the COVID-19 pandemic for almost two years.

That night in Galway, for me, was the true *Querist*. On stage I was a queer-voguing-Irish-step-dancer dancing for Queer and Trans Irish people. Six years later, I still have an open invitation to return. *The Querist* was also my PhD presentation performance. However, as an audience member commented afterwards, it appeared as though I had developed a language that only came into being as the show faded to blackout and bows. This was my intention. The show was designed to feel like a piece of reflexive documentation on a lived process, curated for an academic dance theater.

I have never since performed this piece. Prior to production I danced the first 10 minutes of the piece at the Mermaid Dance Platform in Greystones, a suburb south of Dublin accessible by DART train. This was not deliberate and nor was the fact I would never again perform Step&Vogue in front of an audience. I simply left Ireland, left my PhD and left dancing. Then, the pandemic happened. Some Irish choreographers requested lessons on Step&Vogue, but there was no opportunity to create a community around this, so I turned them down. As I write someone in Dublin has just reached out on Facebook to ask if I am still teaching Vogue in Dublin or if I know of any classes they could take, despite the fact that I only taught one workshop there in 2017. I do not know what any of this means or what it was all for, and it feels okay. Celso, my Vogue Mother, has disappeared and despite years of trying I still have not been able to find her. Neither have I been able to find the words or the dance to process this. Hate devours, and it has taken someone precious to me.

From 2013 to 2017, many people from professional choreographers, arts administrators, teachers and academics explained the "game" I needed to play in order to be a successful choreographer. It seemed to me that if I were to continue playing the game of capitalism after all my study and research on resistance to capitalism via anti-colonialism, anti-racism and anti-homophobia, then I would rather do so from a more financially privileged position than that of an academic, artist or activist. I would become a software engineer.

Summary

In *The Querist* I sought to create a dance about the human–technological encounters that have shaped the history and practice of Irish step dance. I do not claim thereby to have accomplished anything for the audience or for society at large. However, I know that I felt my way through it all and I share that experience here. This piece also allowed me to map for myself the objects and power dynamics at play in my dance, and to teach me how to play with them.

This chapter began with some words of caution about autoethnographic practice-based researchers working with traumatic histories and traditions. I then lay out my rationale for using Berkeley and his text, *The Querist*. Berkeley served to facilitate a Critical Whiteness Studies perspective on my dancing and the present research. I also gave some consideration to how the philosophies of materialism and immaterialism inform this work and how the posing of philosophical questions can be embodied via the fashion poses of Vogue dance.

Next, I discussed the insights that I gained into dance practice during my residency at UCD, which taught me to feel motion through my hands. As an Irish step dancer, hand movements must be carefully considered and gesture, space and effort must feel creatively meaningful. At Iveagh Fitness in Dublin I developed the etudes that would become the basis of the present work. These exercises stood at the axis of fitness, colonial balletic style, Irish step dance and Vogue/Ballroom House. I concluded this section by summarizing the emotional awakening I experienced at MoKS in Estonia. At this time, I realized that feeling the past through history and tradition had transformed the psychometric encounter into a choreography that would help shape my choreo-destiny.

Finally, I discussed the production of The Querist and its aftermath. This performance is best watched in order to be understood. Above, I explained the human–technological encounters that inspired the creation of this show with some description of how I used them and what they meant to me. This production culminated in a nightclub performance in Galway where I could finally Step&Vogue my research. This was the ultimate goal of my research, not the creation of a dance production—although the experience of creating *The Querist* was essential to my growth towards these ends.

The Querist did not plumb the depths of intimate violence as that term did not come to me until much later—five years later. My capacity to grasp and to feel these things for myself through empathetic and sympathetic means would take many seasons of growth and decay to develop. It would also take another identity; it would take *AngelAI*.

Chapter Five:

AngelAI

[A jig, a side step leading with the left leg]
Cut heel and toe, and heel and toe and
Heel and toe, heel and toe and
Jump, kick, hop back-234
Hop, hop back, hop back-234

This chapter presents the final arguments of this thesis by means of an analysis of my second major work, *AngelAI*. I had originally planned to title this work *The Calceologist*, or the one who studies shoes. I was quite pleased with myself when I discovered this salient and obscure word, and I regret that another title supplanted it. Angels and AI have in common the profound tendency to disrupt lives, something that, for reasons that will become clear, I believe justifies this substitution.

AngelAI stands for a return to the first "identity" of An Draoí. Neither *AngelAI* nor An Draoí are English-language names. An Draoí is Gaeilge, and AngelAI is Pascal-case (a style of writing code) for computer programming languages. Although *AngelAI* consists of words intended to be readable to English-speakers, programming languages are interpreted and/or compiled for machines, which gives them a sense of being a "foreign" language. In the context of my dance, Gaeilge and other programming languages do not represent some sort of exotic "other". Rather, they reflect aspects of my identity despite my lack of oral fluency in either (I am not a fluent speaker of Gaeilge and coding languages are generally not spoken). Nevertheless, I express myself in these languages and have come to understand the world through them.[46]

The Psychometrist's penchant for handling technology and deriving knowledge and awareness from this contact (which, depending how you do so, can itself be understood as a kind of "technology") is the theme of *AngelAI*. This work can be taken as an answer to the questions posed in *The Querist*. In this work I perform the role of a Queer Romani man facing a terrifying technological future and the global rise of fascism through online dis-/mis-information, a working-class technologist afraid of losing his job to AI and a dancer afraid of forgetting his sense of self in his body in an increasingly toxic world. *AngelAI* can be summarized as the ultimate question: where are we going vis-á-vis who are we becoming? This enormous yet at the same time pragmatic question has prompted many through the ages to summon for divine aid. In Judeo-Christian communities the hopeless often invoke angels—beings who, according to Biblical canon, see further beyond the next bend than humans and who guide humans towards the light. With each knock of my foot upon the floor in *AngelAI* I issue my own desperate cry for help so that I may know where to take my next step.

I begin this chapter with an invocation of Sara Kali, the patron saint of the Romani people who has supported our journey through time and the darkness of history. I go on to summarize my findings and to situate this project within the broader context of technofeudalism, an evolution of earlier colonial practices that employs digitized methods to achieve mind/body control and the dis- and re-placement of people. In the same way that Berkeley's *The Querist* focused my last production, my lived experience with technofeudalism focuses my psychometric explorations and

---

46 I also speak Spanish to a level of fluency, and have studied German and French. However, these languages have not been part of my self-expression, self-identification and evolution in the way that Gaeilge, Romanes and coding languages have.

awakening to intimate violence in *AngelAI*.

Next, I recount the development of *AngelAI* during my years working as a web developer while researching my Romani identity. I focus on three places that were significant for the development of *AngelAI*: NYU Tisch Department of Dance in the East Village of New York, Pumpkin Hollow in Upstate New York and Northwest Clare in the west of Ireland. At NYU Tisch my studio practices were re-ignited and my Village dancing was renewed as I experienced a sense of homecoming, claiming space and my body again. In Pumpkin Hollow this dance was refined. In County Clare, my stepping was reborn.

Finally, I share the program of *AngelAI* and a story that I told during the performance. The major difference between *The Querist* and *AngelAI* is that in the latter performance my psychometric dance dropped into the feet and legs as I returned to being an Irish step dancer. This chapter concludes with a consideration of the aftermath of this production and the new sense of community I gained as a consequence of it.

On Kalipen in Irish Step Dance

Sara Kali![47] *We have been here from the beginning,*
When you taught us to dance as time itself[48]
Upon the minds of men, again, again.
By stomp, by our step, by chakra, our wheel[49]
We went west, o'er mountains, through the desert[50]
To lands where white turned time into darkness.[51]

In dance there's a frequently neglected
Violent aspect.[52] *I know, I see, I feel*
As an Romani Irish step dancer
Collisions, coercions are core to form.
Bangs, trebles, stomps land controlled cruelty
Upon the floor, trained by years. It is strange
To see the earth and want to beat it—hard.
Or is it our destiny to drum time?

I, a storyteller, also listen
To the cries of feet: slavery, torture
Paradoxically private commons,[53]
Phenotypic races,[54] *Atlantic Worlds:*

---

47 Sara Kali is the patron Saint of many Roma and Sinti people.

48 Referring to the myths of the Hindu Goddess Kali, who is said to represent time.

49 Since 1971, the flag of the Romani people has been the Romani chakra, or wheel. Romanes, the Romani language shares linguistic roots with Hindi in Sanskrit.

50 Referring to the westward migration of the Roma from the region we now call Rajasthan.

51 In Romanes, kali is feminine not for time but for a woman who is dark-skinned.

52 Inspired by Kate Millet's observation in *Sexual Politics*: "Sex has a frequently neglected political aspect," see Kate Millett, *Sexual Politics* (Columbia University Press, 2016).

53 I refer to Linebaugh & Rediker's *The Many Headed Hydra* (2013).

54 Referring to Ndiaye's assessment of the evolution of race as a method of discerning class or religion to phenotype, see Ndiaye 2022.

A Timedancer's Study of Irish Step Dance

Journeys taken from home to not-your-land.
The historians shout the past is gone
So we think our traditions are lost
And we forget the hatred that endures.

How did we move here? What world of things could
Queer a Romani Irish step dancer?
Intimate violence: impact-driven dance.

Paraphrase

Dance has a violent aspect that is often neglected. I know this because I am a Romani Bashaldó[55] harper and an Irish step dancer; collisions and coercions are core to my art. From my Romani family I inherited pulses and rhythms of the road that are thousands of years old, keeping with time in all its unrelenting ferocity. Every touch, every stomp on the ground re-asserts the right to feel, to exist in the face of the convicted Nazi officer who lived two streets over from our town of Independence in Seven Hills, the Ku Klux Klan, which tortured people of color when they moved into our city and white gadje (non-Roma) gypsy lore-ists who stalked families like mine in southern Ohio a century ago (Brown 1972) and who continue to control what people in academia and beyond hear when I say, "I am Roma." In *Romanes* and *Sintitikes*, the Romani and Sinti languages, language is coded in movement. Every sound is a celebration *Romanipen* (Romani-ness) and *Kalipen*, or Blackness as expressed in *Romanes*. We call each other *Kalé*, or the dark people, and have only begun to reclaim what was stolen and to celebrate our sacred Blackness in English.

As my family danced our Irish-American heritage, my Irish

---

[55] Meaning "musician", this is the name many Romungre took a century ago in the mid-west of the United States. Our Romani sub-group is well known for its musicians and dancers.

dancing masters molded my body to move according to a lineage centuries old. I was taught to land every bang, treble and stomp with a controlled cruelty upon the floor and gesture that echoes in the body. This movement felt as distinctly Irish to me as *Gaeilge*, the language I so often heard. It is an unusual impulse to see a floor and want to beat it hard. It is stranger still to beat it, make a dance of it and—in the case of Irish dance—to weave the pounding of shoes on the ground into threads of overlapping, dizzying gesture.

As a historian, I understand this violence and where it comes from. At the start of my academic career over ten years ago I studied through performance fashions of torture, intellectual justifications for colonization and slavery, the privatization of the commons in the early modern Atlantic world (Linebaugh and Rediker 2013) and the ordering of its people based on phenotype (Ndiaye 2022). As I studied this unburied past it expanded the meaning of my practice as a white-passing cisgender male step dancer living with disabilities who learned to dance from my Irish-American, QTBIPOC[56] and Romani families. At the beginning of my doctoral studies my goal was to better understand how Irish step dance evolved in a historical perspective and how people in Ireland experienced their bodies, selves and communities. I had a suspicion that the existing narrative was incomplete and warped by nationalism and that the contributions of Afro-diasporic peoples to the development of impact-driven dance *on both sides* of the Atlantic remained largely un-excavated in academic contexts. I had a hunch that a story of Blackness was yet to be told in the scholarship on this artform. As I kept dancing, situating myself in traditional and experimental Irish step dance choreography, violence and counter-violence revealed something much more intimate than academic inquisition could; I discovered an impact-driven dance based on oppression and a modernity that constantly re-enacts, subverts and heals itself from ongoing disruption in a world still moving through colonial

---

56 Queer, Trans, Black, Indigenous People of Color.

A Timedancer's Study of Irish Step Dance

and capitalist choreography. I discovered myself as a Romani man. I felt blood lineages of which I was not aware. I found where I wanted to go in my steps.

Dancing under Techno-lords

What is the future of impact-driven dance? This project has focused on the early modern evolution of the form and its intimate violences under colonialism, racism and slavery. What is currently happening to the form, what is its future and how does it connect to its past? The concept of "Technofeudalism" has gained currency in the last six years and may supply a framework for posing these questions. Among the many claims of Technofeudalism, which include the death of capitalism itself, is the suggestion that tech platforms constitute the new privatized commons and that they can be understood as colonized lands ruled by a small group of techno-lords (Varoufakis 2024). The emergence of Artificial Intelligence, its domination of investment in the tech industry and its potential to disrupt society for profit in novel ways (e.g. through the centralization and commodification of consciousness itself) makes questions of autonomy, embodied freedom and what it means to be human all the more urgent. AI assisted by virtual realities and other rapidly evolving, immersive technologies may normalize the abdication of the body to digital processes, posing new threats to the survival of dance and embodied knowledge. As an impact-driven dancer this fills me with worry as in my own tech work I have seen how these technologies move continually from being "open sourced" (free and available to all) to being kept in the hands of the few. While there are undoubtedly many conveniences for the general public made available through consumer technology, what happens when the essence of what it means to express oneself through one's body is appropriated and controlled by the wealthy?

Indigenous communities such as the Roma have been able to resist colonial threats many times before, but what of those westerners who lost most of their indigeneity on the long road through Romanization (Roman conquest), Christianization, feudalism, the formation of nation-states, colonialism, racism and the industrial revolution? As the performance arts have become less profitable in American culture, in New York City I have seen music, dance and performance almost disappear entirely from daily life. Where once I saw street performers, public concerts and spontaneous song and dance in public places, now streets are filled only with the sounds of traffic. There are fewer shows in public parks and more conformity in style and self-expression in public spaces, grocery stores, subway trains and on sidewalks. Many arts institutions are closing, such as the Christopher Street studios of the American Tap Dance Foundation where I developed my work over the course of years. As an embodied technologist, I fear that the systems replacing these institutions exist to profit not by taking people into their bodies, but out of them. Meanwhile, the cultures and communities who still preserve a connection to body, community and land will be further exoticized and marginalized. Without dance and our connection to the land, we are primed for digital surveillance, online hate, social engineering, AI theft of intellectual property and mental illnesses. Impact-driven dancers, meanwhile, are primed for tech "disruption" since their dance is a dance of the disrupted—a dance created by those who were driven from their homes, forced to work (and die) in factories or in slavery. Impact-driven dance psychometrically inspects the truth in the body as it makes contact with the world, moving to a new, better one using the patterns and rhythms of the dance. The impact-driven dancers of tomorrow will have to find a way.

There is another part of technofeudalism and does not assume that colonialism—or empire for that matter—ended in the Age of Revolutions. McKinsey Global Institute found that, "Despite the rise of digitization, intangibles are just 4 percent of net worth: they typically lose value to competition and commoditization, with notable exceptions" (Woetzel et al. 2021). Only 4% of global wealth derives from "intangibles" like technology, while, "Two-thirds of global net worth is stored in real estate and only about

20 percent in other fixed assets." (Ibid.) Those other 20 percent of assets include government and corporate-owned infrastructure, buildings and land. This means that the world's economies have never stopped putting a price on land, which has never ceased to be the most valuable asset. As global inequality rises, McKinsey observed that in the last twenty years, three-quarters of all the wealth created came not from savings and investment, but from valuation gains—that is, by increasing the value of property holdings (Mischke et al. 2023). Economics aside, what this data is telling us is that despite all the noise and excitement around social media, AI, crypto-currency and virtual reality, land remains as the most valuable asset to price, own and control. As the population of the planet continues to soar alongside inequality and warfare (whether cold, hot or cyber) fought over land, suddenly the colonialism of the 16th to 19th centuries no longer appears so distant. Our fears about technology are a distraction from the real threat to the well-being of humanity; a threat that has deep roots in a past that we are told is remote from the present. We must also consider the long history of corporations and colonial enterprises. The London Corporation founded the colony of Londonderry, the Massachusetts Bay Company founded the colonies of Massachusetts, the Virginia company founded the state of Virginia and so on. As corporations, especially financial institutions, continue to buy up homes, farmland, forests and land, colonialism acquires a new dimension of terror powered by AI.

The connection between impact-driven dance and the ongoing theft of land and resources struck me while I was taking a break from my doctoral studies and working as a founding software engineer at Fortune Media (of the Fortune500). Though I had left behind my research, I was still confronted by the living legacies of such things as the transfer of land from Indigenous Americans to settlers; the theft of natural resources from people of color; the denial of Romani existence and the denial of their human rights; and the expropriation of land from Irish Gaelic families by British settlers in the 17th century (Ohlmeyer 2012). Around this time I began to face an ongoing, high-profile attempt by my landlord to strip me of housing rights and to displace me from my long-term home on Gay Street in Greenwich Village (Green 2022; Ostadan 2023), facilitated by the neoliberal destruction of housing rights in New York City and New York State. Current events make the past present and lead me to realize the ongoing significance of impact-driven dance. As the wealthy try to steal my home, I try to abandon my body, my dance and my research so that I could fit into their corporate tech world. At the same time, the embodied pulses I inherited from my family and dance teachers are renewed and continue to sustain me. As I have lived with no heat, no electricity and no water during the winter in an apartment held up by shoring on the verge of collapse, while my life is threatened by break-ins and crime facilitated by my landlord—to say nothing of psychological torture—the choice to feel, to be and to understand my own mind and body continues to be more essential than ever before.

The Village of New York has long been a haven for Roma and Sinti people. Two elders in my community live here, although one was recently displaced from his home and business owing to the pandemic and post-COVID government tax policy. The Village also has a history of being a refuge for free African-Americans under Dutch, English and American rule. New York sits on the unceded lands of the Lenape people, or Lenapehoking whose pathways are written into the map of New York City. Impact-driven dance forms are not lost in some distant, un-relatable past. They are continually looking for lost land. It is language articulated in the rupture between sole and earth that defines life for so many in the early modern to post/modern eras and that so uniquely situates impact-driven dance to express this ongoing crisis. Displacement from land—including the displacement of traditionally nomadic peoples like the Roma who do have a connection to land and place—has shaped the violence of Irish step dance.

Development

As artists, we tend to notice what goes missing. As fascists, neoliberals, neoconservatives, capitalists, techno-feudal lords, politicians, activists, academics, CEOs, communists and bureaucrats continually attempt to make our world in their image, it seems it is the writers, poets, musicians, visual artists, craftspeople and dancers whose role it is to mark disappearances. There is an unspeakable horror when something we love or the person inside someone we cherish, vanishes. The scale of loss at the hands of politics and commerce can be felt intimately, nearer than what can be seen or heard. Julie Taylor's *Paper Tangos* (2012) describes the unvoiced terror in another's embrace in milongas as *los desaparecidos* (the disappeared), who were abducted by Argentina's government at that time, were held in the dance.[57] Love and loss carry across the floor with covered eyes as dancers feel the weight inside their partner's chest.[58] I hold this technique inside myself as I step my jigs, reels, slip jigs and hornpipes with my partners from the past and with the children of the dance who will come after me.

In 2020 it was clear what for me had gone missing; I had lost my body. Sometime between leaving my PhD, stopping dancing, becoming a coder and being isolated during the pandemic, I had stopped caring about my body, how it felt and what it was creating. What for a time had seemed like stillness and self-care had turned into immobility and self-hatred. The vitality I had once known was gone. Some well-meaning friends encouraged me to see it as nothing more than the inevitable loss of my youth.

---

[57] Taylor also speaks of the African Argentines who "disappeared" from Argentina in the context of the history of Tango. They were "sent off to the wars where they were promised freedom but met death instead," see Taylor, Julie. *Paper Tangos* (Public planet books) (Kindle Location 922). Duke University Press. Kindle Edition.

[58] In 2004 I helped produce student operas at the Teatro Colon in Buenos Aires and studied tango privately with a dancer named Valeria. She told me to dance *cubierto los ojos* (with covered eyes), using no arms and simply relying on *el peso* "the weight" of my partner's chest against mine.

Then, at 37, I blew out my back by sitting on a chair. For three days movement was excruciating, and I could not get medical care as 60,000 people around me were just then dying alone, scared and in pain in hospitals from COVID-19. I smelled their decaying bodies in the summer air as I walked past the morgue tents. I reflected on the new reality of bodies lost that no one seemed to care about and recalled something told to me two years earlier by a friend and former fellow UL PhD candidate; they told me that already by early 2018 we were screwed as the pandemic response team was dismantled at the American Center for Disease Control. On Twitter and Facebook people said the casualties around me were not real while the president declared NYC a rogue state not deserving of support. I was struck by the casual yet highly strategic bot-fueled crowd-sourced terror of techno-feudalism. It also seemed like almost everything had gone missing. At this time artists were certainly not alone in recognizing the scale of the tragedy taking place, but they were alone in having the right tools with which to witness and record it.

From the years of 2018 to 2020, I did not abandon my research entirely; it kept chewing at my mind. I spent a few years as a speaker and collaborator with the Roma People's Project at Columbia University, benefiting from the kind and generous support of Cristiana Grigore, who guided me past stereotypes and helped me voice the intergenerational traumas that I had not hitherto spoken. I found Roma and Sinti communities existed both locally and in digital communities. I began working on my first academic publication, which was published in print in early 2022. Ironically, as I healed from my intergenerational trauma and as I carried out my research I came to realize that my family had given me some of the greatest blessings of my life. My mother and father made sure I understood computers even though we could barely afford one. They made sure I had dance to stay connected to others and myself. They gifted me with music with which to express myself, learn discipline and, if I needed, busk on the street to make money (which I have done for many years). I learned from them that technology need not supplant human experience by re-asserting capitalism. Instead, technology can be part of a creative experience; my code was my choreography and my choreography was my code. This is an extraordinarily Roma outlook, common for many who seek to resist oppression via innovation. Romani Dance and Irish step dance may be marginal in dance theater, but I no longer viewed this as a problem. My dances are the languages of my life and they open me to new experiences on a daily basis. I realized that I did not need to put on a show and sell tickets to be a dancer. I also realized that the process of finding my voice and my story as a writer on weekends, nights and at the work coffee station was guiding me back to my steps. In the silence of the pandemic, all my self-important PhD research about how my dance was connected to my story turned out to be true. My writing guided me back to my body. It was time to dance again.

The Village: 2019–2023

In 2019 while I was binging YouTube-recommended videos, the algorithm showed me Anne Teresa De Keersmaeker's *Violin Phase*. Set to Steve Reich's 1967 minimalist work of the same name, this solo work is part of De Keersmaeker's *Fase, Four Movements to the Music of Steve Reich* (1982), featuring simply-set choreography to compositions from Reich's collections. The video features the dancer, De Keersmaeker, dancing repetitive, iterative steps and body twists on a platform at a crossroads in the woods. The highly percussive nature of the overlapping violins in the piece generated kaleidoscopic, spiraling punches of rhythm in the dancer's body. It felt terribly Irish to me. I was taken aback by De Keersmaeker's footwork, her use of crossroads which are so vital to the history of Irish traditional dance forms, the singing of the birds at the beginning of the video which recalled my piece *When the Rubber Meets the Dirt Road*, the floating out of arms to invisible dance partners in figurations that bring to mind court/

folk dances,[59] and the sheer audacity of dancing to this repetitive 15-minute piece. My Romani techno-witch imagination sprung to life; this dance was a spell.

I cannot remember if it was on a subway platform, in my apartment, on the gym floor or simply in my mind, but I began to step the pattern I was hearing in *Violin Phase*. This was not like the prancing around the gym and the city that had once consumed me, but it was a step forward. It gave me a sense of self in my body, helping me to understand that the economic power I gained as a software engineer was worthless so long as it cost me my personal power. Leaving academic explanation aside for a moment, I just needed to do some steps. The opening pattern the violinist plays feels like it is ten counts, with the fifth note held in syncopation in a way that feels all the more syncopated for the fact that we cannot tell what meter we are in or even if the melody and harmonies we are hearing are going to take us anywhere. Based on this, I laid down a five-step dance pattern alternating from right and with left legs in front. This pattern started with the right foot forward in fifth position, arms at the sides and standing on the balls of the feet. The left back foot steps down then the right foot lifts slightly and steps down before again the left foot lifts up. As it comes down the right foot comes up into a cut, that is the right heel comes up to the left hip with the knees together. Next, the right foot comes down again and the left foot lifts. As the back foot is placed down again the right foot swings out pointed to the side. As the right foot places behind the left the pattern begins again. This was the beginning of my *Fiddle Fase*.

I played with this pattern in endless repetition for years. It was a rhythmic chant, a spell, a curse, a credo, an impulse, a fidget, a salve and a disruption of disruption. In it the chronospheres of many worlds I had moved through would become the words of a language that helped me to choreonavigate the world and to find my choreo-destiny. I could feel the end of the piece as I discovered its beginning; I knew one day I would dance these

---

59 I had explored this concept for *The Querist*, but cut it at the last minute.

steps in an entire composition. I came to know this through the simplicity of repetition—which I could only physically bear to do for 20 seconds; the dancing was the knowing. The fact that one day I would have to do this pattern in some form for 15 minutes would reflect the insurmountable crises around me. There is something ghastly about having to do the same thing over and over again. For Irish step dancers, who typically dance "full out" for a maximum of 2.5 minutes, this appears inhuman, involuntary and entirely unnecessary.

Fiddle Fase felt like exercise and physical training. In my time as a student and competitive Irish step dancer under Donny Golden in Bay Ridge, Brooklyn and Mineola, Long Island, I would practice dance exercises designed to break down elements of Irish step dances and to aid in physical conditioning and stamina. These same exercises influenced dancer and choreographer, Jean Butler, in the creation of her Irish dance workout video (Butler 2005), which consists mostly of exercises intended to help dancers develop technique. Butler's video influenced both my Irish step dancing rehearsals and my Step&Vogue practice. The pattern I created for *Fiddle Fase* alludes to one of Butler's routines. *Fiddle Fase* became a barometer of my physical fitness, testing my calf strength, my focus and how far I could get through the music before having to stop.

As I danced, it appeared that something new was present: a sensation and response to my movements and what they felt through the world. A new old world was developing around and inside me which I came to know as Romanipen and Kalipen. In my Irish-ness, I grasped the Gaeilge word *neart* (energy) and its potential for holding onto what once grew inside me as I stepped with the Irish community.[60] Alongside the terms *chi*, *kundalini* and *prana*, I searched for an Irish word that could capture this experience. *Neart* is an old Irish word for strength which is also found in other Celtic languages. Academic and

---

60 In the north of Ireland, *neart* in the Donegal dialect means "plenty" or "abundance". My application of this word in my dance is only a suggestion.

spiritual associations aside, any Irish step dancer will agree that the one thing Irish step dance requires above all is strength. The power, vitality and ever-spiraling energy in my dance, *mo neart* (my strength), began flowing in me unexpectedly in 2019 when, as I was settling into my first full-time tech job, YouTube recommended that I watch Anna Teresa De Keersmaeker's *Violin Phase*.

Other time-loops also seemed to come full circle. I began to rent studio space at the American Tap Dance Foundation (ATDF) on Christopher Street—near the pier where I once practiced my Irish dance steps and my Vogue. Here I further practiced *Fiddle Fase* patterns both in hard shoes (with noise) and without (bare foot with attempts at making audible impact). On the walls were painted the heroes of tap dance, and in my trance I felt their presence. Out of the corner of my eye I could see my elders watching. In my early days in New York when I used to practice my dance on the pier known as the Frying Pan, I by chance met Tony Waag, the founder of ATDF, in Hudson. While the wider tap dance community in New York City most likely had no idea that I existed (this is probably still the case), I felt nourished by my connection to them in this meeting of traditions of impact-driven dance. Another thread of influence was entering my dance.

There was another loop, meanwhile, that needed closing: my Arts Practice PhD. In the early summer of 2023, the Arts Practice PhD program at UL welcomed me back with patience and understanding. Unfortunately my previous supervisor, Catherine Foley, had retired, but with great kindness Breandán de Gallaí agreed to be my supervisor. He had throughout my previous PhD journey been a mentor and an inspiration to me as a dancer. With my studentship renewed in June 2023 and only a year left of enrollment in my program, it was time to prepare my second major work. I had two options: to perform at the university in November 2023 or in June 2024, and so November it was. This time I called on a chronosphere composed of Seán Curran, NYU Tisch, the East Village, the Dance Research Forum Ireland conference in 2016 and Greenwich Village. I had first met Seán in Cleveland Playhouse Square twenty years ago at a workshop he gave and that I performed in clumsily. A former Irish step dancer, when I moved to New York City Seán weaved in and out of my life: I dated a couple of his former dancers, performed his choreography in my time with Darrah Carr Dance and saw him around town on occasion. During summer the studios at Tisch are empty, and for a few weeks in August 2023 Seán gave me a much-needed residency at the studios of Tisch on Second Avenue. Together Breandán and Seán gave me the courage to consider dancing publicly again in a solo dance work.

At 111 Second Avenue in the Tisch dance studios, my choreography began to come together. The concept of the work would be similar to *The Querist*. At the beginning of the performance I lay beneath a plastic tarp from which I emerged before dancing upon it. The tarp was a platform on which to further explore shoe/ground relationships. For a later piece, I would return to wearing hard shoes. Two things remained certain: *Fiddle Fase* would be in the show and this time I would not be dancing a series of etudes based on a comment by an 18th-century author, but dancing a story about becoming myself. The music to this piece was also assembled during this residency. On my way to visit a healer friend in Williamsburg, Brooklyn for whom I often performed psychic services, I was researching Reich's *Violin Phase* when I discovered that in the early 2000s the piece was given a makeover to become the *Electric Guitar Phase*. On the platform of the L train the music landed in my body and the choreography shifted entirely. Suddenly, smaller movements and gestures meant more, yet felt more playful than ever. I felt my dance shift into the trance of the music.

When I first arrived at the studios to rehearse I met Seán and explained to him the melange of ideas in my mind and in body while I practiced my Romani Step&Vogue warm-up. I was full of pent-up dance. Seán offered me patience, a kind ear and enthusiasm while he listened to me babble and watched a messy and incomplete run-through of my show.

One day when I came in to rehearse Seán let me know he was interested in the minimalist music I was using. Irish step dance and minimalism form an interesting combination. I told him that I was inspired by De Keersmaeker's *Fase*. When I told him this he took me down the hall and around the corner to a small railway-style studio with no windows that at the time was being painted in preparation for the return of students for the fall 2023 semester. He explained that this was where the Dutch choreographer had in fact made *Violin Fase* during her time as a student in the department forty years previous. Seán remarked that it was bold of me to choreograph such a well-known piece by another choreographer, and noted that no one else had touched it since her. Indeed, he believed the time had come to revisit it. I felt the chronosphere I was meant to encounter here.

Pumpkin Hollow: October 2023

"Are you a dancer?" a woman of indiscernible age with black hair asked me. I had just watched Irish language poet Louis de Paor's collaboration with violinist and Irish traditional musician Dana Lyn in the theater of the Irish Arts Center. De Paor was poet in residence in my department, NYU's Glucksman Ireland House. His passion for Irish culture, Gaeilge and the arts was magnetic and contagious. I spoke a *cúpla focal comhghairdeas* (a few words of congratulations) to him, and he corrected my pronunciation. I could not tell if my error was a regional pronunciation or just plain wrong.

I entered the lobby, which was off of West 51st Street in Hell's Kitchen, Manhattan. The audience was eclectic artsy New York, and across the room a couple with a commanding presence caught my eye. The woman with the *gruaig dhubh* (black hair) approached me in my "Kiss me, I'm Irish" t-shirt, suit jacket and jeans. A short conversation later, Maureen Fleming, dancer, choreographer and photographer, told me she wanted to

A Timedancer's Study of Irish Step Dance

choreograph me as an Irish step dancer.

During the next couple weeks I found myself in the apartment of Maureen Fleming and her husband and longtime collaborator Chris Odo off the Bowery in the East Village. They had lived in this quintessential New York artist's loft in the Village since the early 1980s. Late night music and dance jam sessions still echoed off the walls from the days when the neighborhood was full of well-funded arts initiatives, a creative class, greater diversity and heroin. As my limbs hung from Maureen's patented Fleming Elastxx and she taught me to intone the sacred words that reverberated through my body, releasing "the spirals", it occurred to me that this is what I had moved to this overpriced island for all those years ago. After relocating from the Upper West Side to Greenwich Village a few years earlier, I was dismayed to find that the reputation of this neighborhood for creativity was being rapidly undermined as it turned into a theme park for finance bros and tourists. Through Maureen I got a taste of a reality that was being threatened with destruction by developers and a corrupt city leadership. Eight years later Maureen and Chris were driven from that very studio by landlords who only cared about money and not the people who formed the fabric of this neighborhood.

Throughout winter and spring 2014 Maureen and I exchanged dance. I shared my research and knowledge of Irish step dance and Irish and Irish-American culture, and Maureen taught me her idiosyncratic blend of Butoh meets balletic adagio meets performance art. At this time I was in the first year of my master's degree, which was also the year I was undergoing treatment for PTSD. As Irish step dance seemed to unravel for me, Maureen's dance allowed me to fall into a pool of water together with all my lost and found strands. I began to find where I was. I began to heal.

Maureen and Chris would drive me upstate to their farm where the barn had been repurposed as a dance studio and a theater. We spent long weekends and weeks with other dancers, theater makers and members of the local community near Oneonta, New York learning the Elastxx, practicing Maureen's dance methodology and sharing exercises she had learned from the founders of Butoh. During these trips I came to work on choreography. After hours failing to string a choreography together in their barn, Maureen would teach me how to move from my inner being. Something meta was happening for me as I was transported to my being five years old at my first Irish dance competition in a barn with my mother watching and my father recording. Now, Maureen was watching and Chris would record my dance. I was still Irish step dancing, but it was as though my movements had been suspended and slowed by water, by love. In this slow cadence I had the time to meet myself in my kicks, jumps and twists. Moving from my deepest self, I had the space to process all the impact from my life, from my interpersonal relationships and from the dance. The Elastxx taught me how to move from my inner body not just spiritually but physiologically. Maureen's Elastxx method pulls on you instead of you pulling on it, which changes everything. I learned to move from this extended position with my voice taking the temperature of my alignment on all levels. Not only was this process deeply restorative, but I learned how to truly move from the center of my body using the core muscles.

In the Spring of 2015 I was at Maureen's farm, Pumpkin Hollow, on another long retreat. On this occasion I was energized by having just completed my master's degree and submitting an application to a PhD program in the west of Ireland, at UL. The idea of carrying out Arts Practice research in Ireland inspired movement and the invention of dance pieces. I created *When the Rubber Meets the Dirt Road* and *Monkey Tale,* planting the seeds of the dance that I ultimately wished to create. As the ideas came together for my PhD proposal, a hermeneutic loop was opened. For the next nine years I heard again and again the beginning, middle and end of the sentence I spoke that week with Maureen and Chris.

In early October 2023, I arrived at their farm, Pumpkin

Hollow, to work on my show. Part of my PhD journey began with them, and it made sense to finish it there as well. Maureen was a fabulous dance doctor, and watching her work awakened my own passion for the theater and for experimentation in dance. The focus of my week would be developing *Fiddle Fase*. My show was to take place next month and I was terrified that I would not be able to pull off 15 minutes of Irish step dancing—15 minutes dancing on the balls of my feet would undoubtedly need a powerful finale.

"Move from the perineum, feel the spirals," she would say. In a gutsy moment I decided to begin the first five-minute movement of the piece using the leaning technique I had discovered next to the wedding barn in MoKS, Estonia. I had used this technique in the opening of *The Querist*, and it made sense that *Fiddle Fase* should also begin in this manner. I had begun to call this piece *The Court*. Dancing in the middle of an empty stage I pictured my choreography as a choreonavigation of the early modern colonial imperial court, something which I believe we are still moving through and being moved through today. Though this risked becoming too intellectual, Maureen knew all the hacks to get dancers immediately back into their body and moving from their essence. If I was going to spend five minutes moving slowly to this punchy, layered electric guitar, I would have to commit to it—and the best way to commit was to feel it deeply.

At the end of the week we took a number of recordings of the full number, as well as a still of me jumping that I could use for a promotional poster for the show. The picture was perhaps the most difficult thing for me. I was about forty pounds heavier than I was when I had danced *The Querist*, and the idea that I would share with the world, particularly the competitive Irish dance world, a picture of me older and heavier made me feel like a failure. I knew that many dancers would simply not consider me one of them anymore. Insecurities aside, Maureen saw the dance in the picture and the truth that I was really dancing. In the summer as I dreamed myself into this piece, I considered incorporating

Artificial Intelligence and decided to call it *AngelAI*. Seán loved this name, and Maureen pushed me further and said, "you're *AngelAI*! This is a dance of a man who lost his body to technology, and his journey to get it back." Maureen always encouraged me to work with myth as text and subtext. Her approach was inspired by the comparative mythologist Joseph Campbell and his wife Jean Erdman, who was herself a dancer-choreographer. Maureen knew the couple personally, and Campbell had said to Maureen in an elevator after one of her performances, "your dance is your transcendence." I told Maureen that I was influenced by the myth of Icarus, and it became clear that in *AngelAI* I was playing at Icarus, who flew too close to the sun and lost his body. I was less interested in that part of the myth so much as I was in his afterlife. So technology and hubris killed him, now what? It made sense to me that he should have become an angel in the form of technology, in the form of AI.

I became *AngelAI*, and that felt honest. It also was a formidable task that kept me distracted from my body image issues, and the limitations of my movement that came from having more weight than I was accustomed to. It was time to go back to Ireland.

Clare: October-November 2023

As my Aer Lingus flight from JFK was re-routed to Dublin owing to fog, I took a shuttle back to Shannon. The Irish countryside rolled out before me. I felt all the previous trips I had taken to Ireland and micro-trips for my research assemble into a journey. All the weight, regret and excitement around my previous lives in Ireland fell somewhere behind me on the M7 motorway. This time I was able to simply let go into the privilege of being where I am with all the people who I had come to know, and to love. I carried my dance steps with me. I knew a thing or two about them and how I wanted to share them, and that was enough.

Over Irish breakfast at Maria and Michael's home in

Ennistymon (they are no longer based in Estonia) we shared the latest news from our lives and our dance. Dance was inseparable from their lives and the poetry of their speech. A conversation with Maria and Michael was an opportunity to show them that I was practicing what I claimed my work was doing. I was completely full of it. There is a rigor that comes from being close to our friends, particularly when those friends are used to constantly reflecting on the ethics of their behavior on the global stage. There was an ominous visitor that morning. In my years of being their guest I had had a sense that the world was heading in a good direction, and that our research might help with that. This time it was different. Maria was volunteering to help displaced Ukrainians living in Lisdoonvarna. I worried for Palestinian and Israeli friends who had families and friends who died or who were now in danger after the outbreak of war. I worried about the ongoing humanitarian crisis of the Roma and Sinti in Europe and around the world and that our governments would not be able to meet the challenges of today. Maria's collaborators in England had lost their department of performance art studies to bankruptcy on the first day of the fall semester. My news on the state of dance and the arts in New York and the USA was not much better. How do we move from here? As propaganda spreads online, what is the future of research, politics and our ability to connect as humans?

It was mid-October and for the next six weeks I lived in a house by the sea in Lahinch, County Clare. When I returned to Irish dance class in New York City in 2006, I had written in my journal of my dream of living in Ireland. I would wake up in my own house, go swimming in the rejuvenating, frigid waters of a lake or ocean, dance in a church-turned-dance hall, do some work before joining a trad session with my friends. In the following years, I failed to attain this idyllic fantasy—indeed for most Irish people this dream remains financially impossible. Now that I was finishing my PhD, I decided to rent a house near my friends who lived in and around Ennistymon, County Clare and at last experienced living for a short time the life I had wanted for so long. I would wake up in the early hours of the morning to work out overlooking the moody Atlantic Ocean. Most days I swam before heading back to my holiday rental to cook breakfast and get ready for the dance studio. I would have to be home by 2:30PM to start my tech day job, so it was a long day.

I developed my work alone in Maria's dance studio in the Burren Artist Studios in Lisdoonvarna. Rainbows, cliffs and hawthorn berries provided a backdrop to practicing *AngelAI*. The landscape, the land and the community flowed into my step dancing, resolving for me the matter of what to do with my hands. My legs seemed to carry all of this, along with what I psychometrically perceived and imagined. I had planned for this production to focus on impacts between feet and floor, but what would I do with my Step&Vogue and with the Romanipen that flowed so often through my spine, arms and head? Another question also lingered; I was confident I would call my dissertation "Intimate Violence: Feeling Impact", but what was I feeling impact in or from? What will be in the name of my dance and what did I hope to accomplish from naming it? Clearly, I decided I was feeling impact in Irish step dance. But why? I chose this title not just because of where I started in dance but because it felt like there was some sort of ending to the way I related to that identity. On the edge of Europe in the "Wild Atlantic", I experienced not just a homecoming to my life in Ireland. I also said goodbye to a journey of becoming at home in myself. I did not need to Step&Vogue, pose questions or feel in any way at odds with my queer, American, disabled or Romani identity anymore. I could simply be here, do my Irish dance steps and be all of these things. Once this project is complete I will be able to explore more movements and how they intersect or do not with myself. *AngelAI* is Irish step dance, and that is that.

Some days I would go to dance at the Comhaltas-run *Teach Ceoil* (Music House) in Ennistymon with Maria and her dance collective. There I experienced the sense of community, sharing and exploration that I had long yearned for. The Music House happened to be in an old church. Most days Daire would come, carrying forward her sister's legacy of cherishing the choreography of life. No walk through the bog or over the stones of the Burren, no smell of the wilderness beneath our feet was unwelcome. Together we felt each element ripple through the cold wood floor onto the rafters. When it was my turn to lead the session, I taught Irish step dance through a series of images that I had assembled from a combination of Maureen's Butoh, our Ennistymon dance collective and my psychometry. I drew on images and ideas that had come to me in the course of my practice and that I felt best captured the process of psychometric awakening in Irish step dance. The most useful to me and for the other dancers was the concept that our feet carry two different timelines—one a history of walking barefoot or in light slippers on the balls of our feet, and another a history of heavy shoes that drive us to walk into our heels, roll into the foot and then push off from the toes. These are thus two chronospheres that intersect in each foot, and the Irish step dancer masterfully maneuvers both. Holding these timelines in their bodies, my somatic companions discovered Irish step dance choreography naturally without me having to teach them specific heel and toe steps according to the typical manner. Each gesture of exploration brought us closer together and increased our awareness of the precious things that existed between us.

Maria would also come to the studio to watch me in that moment of my dance—without explanation. Choreographically this prompted me not to take anything I was doing for granted. Maria considered every one of my movements. Any embodiment I did not truly intend was either explored further or returned to the ether. Maria held many images that stretched into stories from those she had met in her somatic practice. My own orchesography of psychometric human–technological encounters was thus easy for her to adopt and meet in counterpoint. This felt like direction, and she helped me—as Breandán put it after one performance—come out from underneath the tarp.

Under Maria's gaze the hard shoe piece dropped, quite literally. I began this piece by telling a story as I put on my hard shoes before entering a low squat. With my elbows on my knees, I gazed at the floor in front me for a moment. This reminded Maria of a Mayo farmer who had once said at a community meeting, "as sure as my elbows are on my knees," when making his point. I told Maria that my surname came from Mayo, nearby or on Achill Island. My apparent connection to this farmer through his expression was a smaller gesture, the closing of a time loop started by great-great grandfather John Browne.

Maria also joined me for my three days of tech, providing me with sliced pear and rice cakes, a keen eye for visual detail and respect for the theatrical format. The incredible crew patiently helped me to realize a vision beyond what I had imagined possible. In the few theatrical works I have created in my lifetime I have always relied on darkness, shadow, silence and visual ambiguity. In my experience unclaimed spaces left room for the unseen to make a spectacle of themselves. Perhaps the most visually striking of absences became apparent on the first day when I had laid my worn tarp down, upstage left as Pius the lighting designer turned on the sleek, new lighting grid and two jagged circles landed centerstage, both overlapping in the middle, one illuminating the majority of the tarp. Michael later came to tell me after the show that he appreciated the optical illusion of the tarp appearing to be simply an extension of the rippled circular lights. When it began to make noise and move his assumptions about what was on the floor was unsettled. Maria called these two lights, which would return in force for the finale of the piece, *Fiddle Fase* turned *The Court*, my angel wings.

Much to my surprise, I had found joy in choreographing for the theater. This was not borne out of any certainty that my work was doing anything particularly spectacular or effective. Rather it came from the experience of being creative with other people. My stage manager Aoife, an Irish step dancer herself, kept us on schedule and helped me to keep my steps in time. Breandán, meanwhile, offered a keen eye for choreography and technique, helping me to bring double-hops, cuts and leaps into clearer focus. Maria's direction taught me passion and expertise for form, pacing and audience interaction. While I appeared to be dancing a solo show, a céilí of embodied and intellectual hands led me across the floor. Now, it was showtime.

Production

The program from the November 16, 2023 in the Irish World Academy of Music and Dance Theatre One contains the following verses:

The earth, shaken
Tossed in the air
The floor fell away
While I'm still there

Drawn of Dedalus
Fallen from the sky
Angel of Icarus
An AngelAI

Along with the following credits:

The Floor

Music and Choreography by Russell Patrick Brown

The Sabot

Choreography by Russell Patrick Brown, with excerpts from Riverdance and Donny Golden's competition choreography

The Court

"Electric Guitar Phase" by Steve Reich
Performed and recorded by Dominic Frasca
Choreography by Russell Patrick Brown

Technical Management: Alan Dormer

Lighting: Pius McGrath

Sound: Juhani Konttinen

Video: Scott Robinson

Stage Management and Irish step dance consulting: Aoife McGarry

Costume: Leggings, Grishko; blue sleeveless shirt, Lululemon

Russell Patrick Brown is an Irish traditional step dancer who learned to move his legs from Tessie Burke, Niall O'Leary and Donny Golden, hold his arms from members of the House of the LaBeija, open his techno-heart from his Roma and Sinti family and kumpania (community) and feel spirit from Rev Dr Patricia Bell, Mavis Pittilla, Maureen Fleming and Maria Kerin.

Towards the middle of the production, I tell the following story:

Have you heard the story of sabotage?

I was visiting a friend in Munich. He's a German Sinto, a Spanish Zincalo and a fellow gypsy. I was telling him about my obsession with shoes—wooden shoes that is—and he asked me if I knew the story of sabotage.

He said about 200 years ago during the Industrial revolution the French military would go door to door forcing farmers and tradespeople at gunpoint to abandon their homes and go work in the factories.

There, they faced long hard hours, dangerous conditions and they wore wooden shoes.

In resistance, they would take their wooden shoes, their clogs, their sabot and kick in the machines. This became known as sabotage.

Later that day we went together to Dachau, where most of his family had been killed during the Holocaust. Then, I found out they'd been wearing wooden shoes.

The show ran for approximately a half hour.

Aftermath

We finished our Thanksgiving Friday-night taco party and headed for the golf course. My show ended a week ago. My spiritual friend and mentor Patricia had left, my sister had arrived and I was to head back to New York in a few days. It was time to celebrate with the community that had so often welcomed me back and back again to Clare. I grew up with Romani nomadic traditions, and while my family did travel as tourists, this was never as enjoyable or meaningful as returning to visit those we had met on our journeys. In the Irish traditional music world Clare is considered holy ground with the Willie Clancy Summer Week taking place there every year at Miltown Malbay. Céilí and set dancing were popular in Clare for generations with the highly respected fiddler Martin Hayes and other traditional musicians coming from the county. My friends[61] incorporated this history into lives spent stepping on the land on two legs among other dancers, occasionally with a hop, twist and a stamp. I brought this community together for Mexican food the day after a colonial American holiday.

As we jumped the stone fence onto the golf course in the darkness of the night, trying not to fall and dirty our clothes, a friend remarked to me that this would make a brilliant party piece. Long ago during my first period living in Ireland I played the keyboard for the Killarney Musical Society's production of *Carousel* (Rodgers & Hammerstein). An 18-year-old Jessie Buckley starred in the musical before going on to become a West End and Hollywood star. The sets were marvelous, my friend Niamh (who got me the gig) played, with the actor's accents being a mix of Kerry and Texas (despite the story being set in Maine). The production was deeply moving. In the hostel I stayed at that week I woke up in my bunk bed to an elderly man staring at me about two feet from my face. He had been sleeping in the bunk

---

61 For their privacy, I will not be naming who was in attendance during this jaunt other than my sister.

beneath me and introduced himself as Morgan from Killorglin. Throughout that week of rehearsal and nightly performance he gave me a much-needed education in banter, jokes and party pieces. The "gift of the gab" is famous in Irish-American contexts and informs stereotypes about what it means to be Irish— stereotypes that were built on racist caricatures of the Irishman and Irish woman popular on the 19th-century American stage (Williams 1996: 118). It lives on in the form of the cereal mascot for Lucky Charms, the Leprechaun and in most American St Patrick's Day costumes. What Morgan taught me, however, was not how to kiss the Blarney Stone, but how to think critically, cleverly, artistically and effectively with my words. I of course did not conjure up a single piece of amusing or insightful discourse with Morgan, so he took care of most of the talking. Fifteen years later, I learned to leave storytelling party pieces to the seanchaí (storytellers). This night in late November in Lahinch my party piece would involve breathing the sea air, walking on tall grassy mounds and trespassing on a golf course built under British colonialism that dominated the best land by the sea.

Splayed out on tufts off enormous grass on the top of a large hill overlooking the crashing waves and town to our left, we began to sing. The songs we sung were funny, touching and locomotive. My sister sang the popular Girl Scout song, "The Princess Pat", which is a rhythmic, catchy tune sung in call and response. The tune originates from the 1917 Canadian WWI regiment of Princess Patricia, who was born on St Patrick's Day in Buckingham palace as the granddaughter of Queen Victoria and daughter of the Duke of Connaught, a province just north of us in Clare, Munster. If anyone knew this at the time of our illegal party occupation, they did not volunteer the information. It was a delightful session.

After an impromptu dance party near one of the holes, we headed back to my rental cottage. On our way my sister and I spoke about our Irish ancestry. Americans have been foraging for ancestral roots in Ireland for many decades, and I typically spare my friends this kind of talk. Tonight however we alighted on the topic of our hereditary surnames, one of which is Quilty. Much to my surprise my friends told me that Quilty was a town just five minutes down the road from where I was staying in Lahinch. In this moment, the coincidence made me feel at home, another time loop of colonialism, immigration and loss closed.

AngelAI derives from the moment when a community helped me to question what remains of us when we collide with the machinery of the world which has been co-opted by the powerful to control our bodies. Our impact-driven dance stages battles of mythic proportions for somatic inquiry. I am doubtful that *AngelAI* will ever be performed again, but I practice it daily. In the steps of my life I discovered my own sabotage, a Sinti and Romani wisdom contained in every collision of my shoe. This collision is also shared by Irish people and African-Americans. I draw on Tyler D. Parry's groundbreaking text on *Jumping the Broom: The Surprising Multicultural Origins of a Black Wedding Ritual* (2020) and the techniques he created to mediate the Romani, Celtic and Afro-diasporic origins of this practice, which my family still carries with it:

> The broomstick wedding is a product of the transatlantic exchange, spurred by European colonization, that spanned the sixteenth through nineteenth centuries. But one must examine the custom from more specific vantage points and consider how the interactions between gender, race, and class contribute to a group's cultural development. By viewing the custom's expressions on both sides of the Atlantic, alongside their distinctions within and between different ethnic groups, we take all groups involved seriously as cultural innovators. Analysis of the marriage traditions of Celts, Romani, and the English on one side of the Atlantic, and those of enslaved people of African descent, Cajuns, and rural white Americans on the other indicates that the custom is undoubtedly most relevant for marginalized peoples. The broomstick wedding's multicultural importance reveals how myth, memory, and history provide important paradigms in studying rituals and their impact on the cultural development and identity

> formations in each community. Each group uniquely practiced the custom, and its pertinence to their cultural identity was a reference point for the outsiders who judged them. (Parry 2020: 9–10)

Parry goes on to say what also matters above all is who carries this tradition, particularly when it comes to those who have gained greater economic and social privilege. Broom-jumping is an important part of Romani, Celtic and African-American culture, and has long been practiced in the dance. It can be understood in terms of an HTE. I intend to further study the Romani associations of this practice so that I can understand not just how others should own it, but how I carry it. In this way, my impact-driven dance through intimate violences involves a personal, ethical responsibility that only I can meet in my dance, whether or not an audience is there to witness it. In the case of *AngelAI*, I met this responsibility alone on stage, but not alone in my life.

The premise for *AngelAI* was for me to play the part of an embodied AI inhabited with angelic consciousness and trained on the data of human–technological encounter, intimate violence and psychometric dance with impact. I perform as an imagined angel entity learning who it is we are. As my mentor Patricia remarked, "What is this angle trying to tell us? It's telling us about how our bodies have been controlled and how to break free." As technofeudalism transforms colonialism by developing digital methods of mind and body control, I offer my dance not just as resistance, but as an inheritance that absorbs its malignant impact and thereby transcends it.

Summary

This chapter explains my return to my doctoral research amid a hostile situation imposed on me by technofeudalism, which I employ as a term to encapsulate a new tech-driven approach to the agenda of corporate colonialism which is designed to benefit the few and control the masses. Technofeudalism is responsible for the ongoing threat to my rights as a tenant in Greenwich Village, an experience that gives me a better perspective on the history of colonialism and how it has impacted and continues to impact people's lives. Colonialism constitutes the primary intimate violence of this PhD—the fact that our connection to the earth around us and all who dwell there has been taken away from us. Impact-driven dance psychometrically dances place, identity and home in an ever-evolving terrain increasingly hostile to life as we know it.

Since withdrawing my doctoral studies and my life dancing, I have lived an idle, tech-controlled life where I choreograph machines and not people, perhaps so that machines can in turn choreograph people. This is where artists mark the losses of modernity. My step dance helped me find my body, which I had forgotten, precipitating my return to dance and returning me to my investigations into the history of materialism in Irish step dance as it helps me to better understand contemporary calamities and threats to humanity and the earth.

Next, I discussed the development of *AngelAI* which followed a similar trajectory to the development of *The Querist*, with settings in the Village of Manhattan, New York City, in Pumpkin Hollow in Upstate New York and in Northwest Clare, Ireland. In the Village I found the tradition of minimalist music and dance through Steve Reich and Anna Teresa De Keersmaeker's *Violin Phase*, which by coincidence involved choreography that De Keersmaeker had developed in the studios that I myself used to create *Fiddle Fase*, in the dance studies of NYU Tisch. This experience allowed me to develop a technique of entering a trance-like state where I could access my neart (energy), an expression of Irish-ness embodied in the rigorous, repetitive stepping of movements over time. In this way, I re-ordered temporalities of traditional dance, their histories and my own timescale of life.

In Pumpkin Hollow with Maureen Fleming and Chris Odo I returned to a place of healing from trauma that has accompanied me throughout my academic journey in dance. The suspension of my movements with the Fleming Elastxx and Maureen's inherited Butoh technique allowed me to investigate what is there in me and in the dance at the meeting of foot and floor. Maureen's dance doctoring helped me break through to what felt like my first real dance production. I experienced a deep sense of community and fellowship in dance in County Clare while living and training in Lahinch, Lisdoonvarna and Ennistymon. My friends Maria and Michael and the community there gave my steps, my neart and an unexpected sense of healing and homecoming. In the face of global catastrophe, this brought *AngelAI* to life.

The production of *AngelAI* itself involved poetry which served to situate the work, as well as a story mid-way through the half-hour show. The majority of the choreography was simply Irish step dance. The act of using Irish step dance as my primary means to tackle the fraught HTEs and intimate violences at hand felt personal yet revolutionary. I proved to myself that the 18th-century materialist history of Irish step dance foremost concerned our connection to the ground beneath us, and all that dwell on it with us. In the aftermath of the performance I came to learn that we have a right to feel ourselves, our past, present and future communities and our connection to the land through our bodies without apology, justification or aid of cartography.

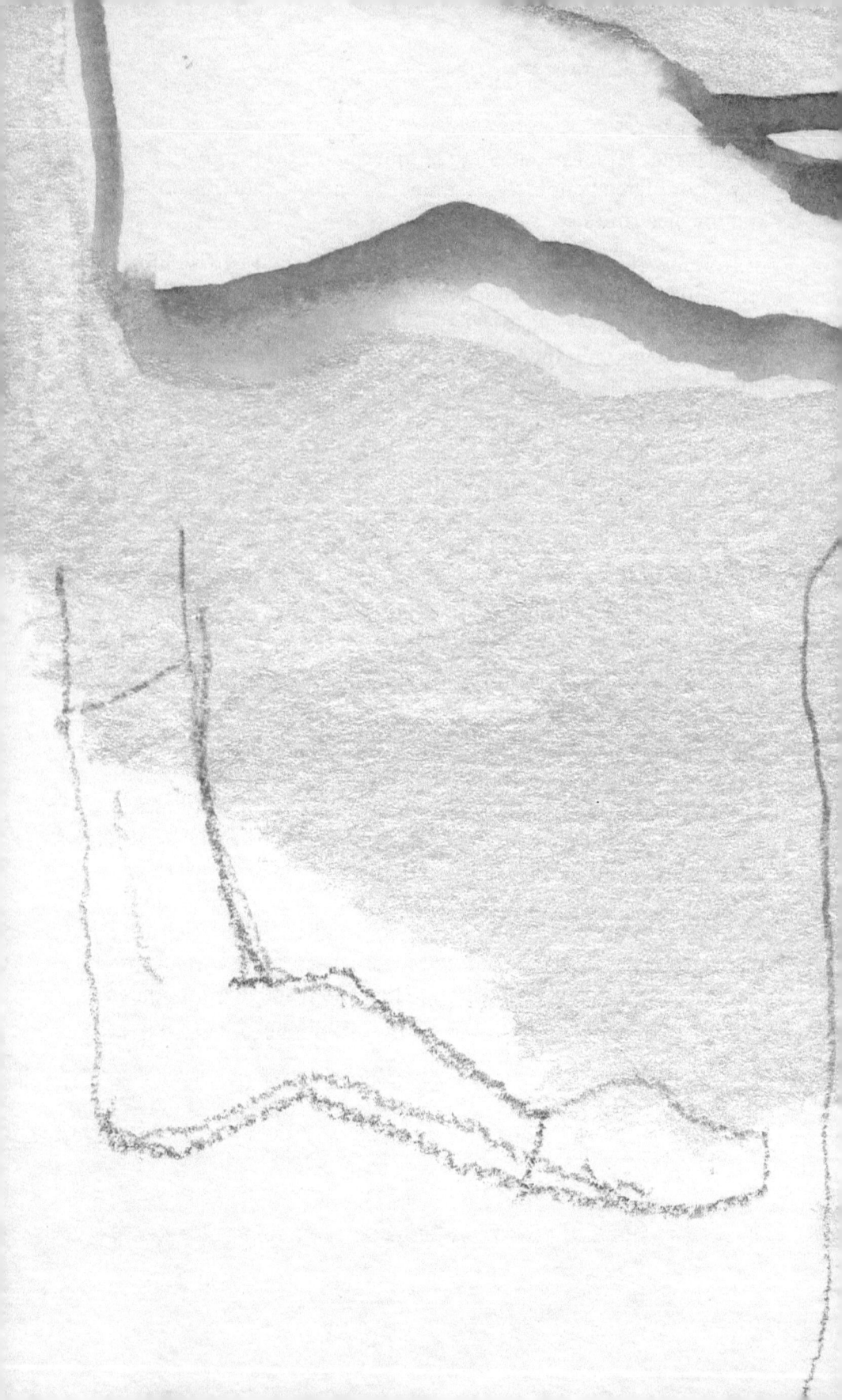

CHAPTER SIX:

Cuir Síos (Conclusion)

On my first visit to Ireland in 2007 people kept giving me cups of tea. Each time my friend Martin's mother placed the hot, bitter brew before me I smiled politely and thought to myself, "this is awful." Still, the mugs kept coming. At that time I did not drink coffee either, so my dislike could not only be blamed on continental variations in preferences for caffeinated beverages. I just did not understand why anyone would want to drink tea. When I was told that Irish etiquette requires refusal of the tea three times before you can accept it, I was really lost. Scones were also highly suspicious to me; they have an uncanny resemblance to lumps of wall plaster and appear to make for very effective door stops. I suggested to my fellow American dance partner at the time that we use our tea time instead to devour our tiny sandwiches and to practice our dance steps, which we did on the floor next to the table that was set out for tea. We made a horrible racket and I later found out we had damaged the floors to the point that they would need replacing, which really went to show I was the worst guest for afternoon tea imaginable.

Over the years the teacups kept coming, but so did something else. In 2008 my fabulous fiddler friend Niamh would fetch a cup of tea at random times so that we could sit down and "natter": have silly, idle chit chat, like when we were deciding if the game of squash we played with tennis rackets should be called "twash" or "squennis." In 2009 my Irish language class at the Irish Arts Center in Hell's Kitchen, Manhattan would have drop-in hours for informal conversations called tae agus comhrá (tea and chats). In 2013 my Irish-American childhood friend Cheryl who had moved to London would tell me that when I was stressed out I should have a "cuppa", sit down, relax and talk about next steps. In 2014 at GIH we would all make cups of tea on breaks and gossip about our classmates. In 2015, my landlady and future friend Ailish would tell me late at night as she leaned out the window to have a smoke after a long day working in collections to "put on the kettle" and grab my deck of tarot cards while we looked at real estate listings around Limerick that we had no intentions of buying. In 2017 as I scrambled to make my choreographer's dream work, Maria would invite me for a cup of tea so that we could have what she called a cuir síos—a putting down of our thoughts and woes, together. In the pandemic I would come to brew tea and stare out the window at nothing in particular. As I write this now with a cup of Barry's tea by my side, I realize that I was not just drinking tea, I was swallowing what it meant to be human. In every natter, chit chat, cuir síos, gossip and silence between friends I decolonized my mind from a nauseating focus on the aspirational and discovered a serenity in the choreography of souls in conversation. Drinking tea is a powerless endeavor, which is what makes it so powerful.[62]

The linguist in *Arrival* ultimately comes to realize that the gift of the heptapods was a non-linear language that unlocked the beauty of her life—past, present and future. Before the credits roll we see her teaching the language in a university setting as she boldly faces the tragedies of life she knows are coming owing to her new alien fluency. With a little imagination and some knowledge of our capitalist world, it is not hard to imagine her in a sequel having been elevated to some sort of celebrity status as the only one who truly understands this mystical language. The rest of the world would demonize her, idolize her or both—just as they did with the heptapods. In my version of the sequel, however, something else would happen. People would come to

---

62 I am aware that tea drinking, particularly afternoon tea, is associated with aristocracy and colonialism. Today, the act of tea drinking in American culture is generally forgotten and most certainly anti-capitalist in its complete lack of productivity.

recognize the non-linear orthography hidden in plain sight in our traditions. Conversations are linear. They have a clear beginning, middle and end. In business, academia and on social media we must use this arrow of communication to be effective and to get what we think we need done. At tea time, other temporal dimensions appear in the dialogue: the times you drank tea by yourself and calmed down, the moments when you added some whiskey to your tea because your friend was sharing good news or the lazy afternoon when someone you love sat by your side in stillness and you sipped—not knowing this would be the last time. These moments slip together, bonded by the beat of what it means to be human. We learn more about each other, we begin to cope with the unbearable and we find our way around ourselves in these traditions. We could say that we are learning to love ourselves and others in these moments, but there are many conditions and requirements that assert themselves in the realm of love. In tradition I think something much more immediate and obvious takes place; we share in life itself. Together, we have lived.

In impact-driven dance I propose that we are dancing because we have lived *here*. In tapping the ground beneath us, slapping our hands together or rapping our knuckles on a table-top we have folded place, our bodies in place and the things we have carried by choice or force into our multi-temporal traditions of being human. We command not just a non-linear, circular sense of time, but an embodied one. When my friends watched me dance, I came into a fullness of myself, embodying all the mixed identities I carry inside me. I am whole. What we carry in our bodies may be unbearable, but we are not alone in carrying our identities through time. Our percussive dance tradition is a creation like no other, and even if we lose it all tomorrow through some disaster or unfathomable new evil form of body control, someone would find the rhythm of life in their body again. They would tap on the futuristic cage around them and no matter how many times they would be stopped—the pulse would spread. Gestures are contagious. Rhythm spreads. When we are down or when we are gone, the weights we carried in our dance now carry us.

At the end of this project, I begin to feel the impact of intimate violence in my step dance. I know that some may think that my psychometric dance with human–technological encounters through Irish step dance provides worthless or fraudulent information, and that is okay. For me and my lineage of impact-driven dancers, what we think and feel when we touch the world is not superstition or subjective nonsense. It is the reason we are alive. As the machines of our world grow ever more powerful, it is worth asking, "do we trust what they think and feel more than what we think and feel ourselves?" What matters?

This text is ultimately my own journey to my choreo-destiny, nothing more or less than that. What is the destination?

- A call to the end of violence in all its forms.
- A call to the end of colonization, that we stop trying to push others out from the land that they are on.
- A call to recognize human agency in technological disruption, and a recognition of the agency of machines in our lives.
- Who we are and how we feel matter matters, that we do not stand behind a scientific method that hides bias behind the supposed objectivity of the perception of machines.
- The freedom to shape my own body and destiny, regardless of broader recognition or lack of it.
- That when violence happens it happens in this time and all times.
- Our ability to feel impact is a way into a non-linear orthography, a new orchesography of the consciousness manifest in this time and all times.

I do not think the dance can do all that, however, it can only carry the truth that I am here in the hopes of these timeless dreams coming true. This suggests that when we approach tradition perhaps we should be concerned less with authenticity, and much more with autonomy. Each Irish step dancer's steps does not present the problem of "tradition," but the need for it. Every dancer must define the past for themselves, for their capacity to do so has a direct correlation to their ability to imagine a new future—and our dreams of the future shape how we understand where we have been.

As I consider the orchesography of the early dancing masters, I think they were on the right path. Dance should be noted, studied and written in addition to being danced. Likewise, dance can teach us how our words are but an orchesography of life itself. It is not just the gestures of the body however that need translation into print—it is the intent and impact behind them. It is my hope that the growing convergence in dance research for studying how we make dance and why we make it, and what it means to us continues to blossom to new frontiers, and to the obvious we have taken for granted. For myself, the future holds a return to being my whole self as a harper, singer, storyteller, acrobat, coder, dancer, composer, choreographer, psychic, medium and whatever else I can throw into the mix. I will be Romani, Irish, Queer, Disabled and whatever other pieces of myself I belong to. Oddly enough, in focusing just on this little corner of dance, I have felt like I was doing all these things. If our impact-driven dance can carry the impossible weight of so many awful things, that means it can also carry more wishes and dreams than we can ever imagine.

Impact-driven dance also aims to restore and maintain agency in traditional dance practice for the communities that most forcefully felt those collisions. Another essential step in this process was brought to my attention by a friend and colleague in dance studies, Emilie Jabouin, whose work contributes to the reclamation of stolen culture. She referred me to Eromose Iacci's graphic novel series, *The Crusaders*, which tells the story of siblings who retrieve pieces of their stolen heritage and return them to their communities (Iacci 2022). Iacci's diligent research on the British Empire's destruction of the kingdom of Benin whose plunder made its way into the British Museum was an awakening to me. His transformation of this legacy into an Afro-futurist creative work about the righting of historical *and ongoing* wrongs was an inspiration. Given that the Roma are Europe's largest ethnic minority and have had a presence there since the Middle Ages alongside other communities of color, we have only just begun to re-thread our histories, lives and practices in Anglophone academic and artistic spaces. In this work I reclaim Romani dances and lives that are continually erased from non-Roma stories, I learn from Irish indigeneity as taught to me by Irish people themselves who navigate post/colonialism within Ireland. I celebrate the Blackness of impact-driven dance that is perpetually whitened and I acknowledge all peoples who have been driven from their ancestral lands by colonialism. I accept the gifts of my mother and father. In capitalism we are trained to own what we enjoy, and in many cases to truly accomplish this whoever brought this pleasure to us must be erased by our own becoming. This is where impact-driven dance subverts this process—you cannot step someone else's impact. Also, when we move from a hyperchronic sense of time, we endure.

Traditions like those in Irish step dance and impact-driven dance as a whole create a place in modernity where who we are, where we have been and where we are going cannot so easily be tossed aside by the vices of humanity. Traditional dance forms prompt us to ask, what are we willing to ask of history? Are we letting what we believe about the limitations of our sources and methods limit what we are willing to ask of dance history? This study assumes that the study of dance is not just an attempt to glimpse the ephemeral, but is a study of that which is most enduring to us: our humanity.

At this moment I can answer for myself, did I know what I was doing all along? Did my ancestors know what they were doing all along when they made these dances? Do all the dancers who will come after me know? Yes, we certainly did, we do and we will.

A Timedancer's Study of Irish Step Dance

Reference List

Adnan, Atif, Allah Rakha, Hayder Lazim, Shahid Nazir, Wedad Saeed Al-Qahtani, Maha Abdullah Alwaili, Sibte Hadi, and Chuan-Chao Wang. "Are Roma People Descended from the Punjab Region of Pakistan: A Y-Chromosomal Perspective." *Genes* 13, no. 3 (March 17, 2022): 532. https://doi.org/10.3390/genes13030532.

American Psychiatric Association. *Diagnostic and Statistical Manual of Mental Disorders: DSM-5*. Washington, DC: American Psychiatric Association, 2013.

Arendt, Hannah, and Amos Elon. *Eichmann in Jerusalem: A Report on the Banality of Evil*. 1st edition. New York, NY: Penguin Classics, 2006.

Patrick Ball. *Celtic Harp, Vol. I: The Music of Turlough O'Carolan*. Fortuna Records, 1983.

Patrick Ball. *Celtic Harp, Vol. III: Secret Isles*. Fortuna Records, 1985.

Banes, Sally. *Terpsichore in Sneakers: Post-Modern Dance*. 1st edition. Middletown, CT: Wesleyan, 2011.

Barad, Karen. "Posthumanist Performativity: Toward an Understanding of How Matter Comes to Matter." *Signs* 28, no. 3 (2003): 801–31.

Barrett, Estelle, and Barbara Bolt. *Practice as Research: Approaches to Creative Arts Enquiry*. London: I. B. Tauris, 2010.

Berkeley, George. *A Treatise Concerning the Principles of Human Knowledge*, 2003. https://www.gutenberg.org/ebooks/4723.

Berkeley, George. *The Querist, Containing Several Queries, Proposed to the Consideration of the Public. By the Right Reverend Dr. George Berkley, Lord Bishop of Cloyne. To Which Is Added, by the Same Author, A Word to the Wise: Or, an Exhortation to the Roman Catholic Clergy of Ireland*. 2nd London edition. London : printed for W. Innys, C. Davis, C. Hitch, W. Bowyer; and sold by M. Cooper, in Pater-Noster-Row, 1750.

Bochner, Arthur P., and Carolyn Ellis. "An Introduction to the

Arts and Narrative Research: Art as Inquiry." *Qualitative Inquiry* 9, no. 4 (August 1, 2003): 506–14. https://doi.org/10.1177/1077800403254394.

Bourriaud, Nicolas. *Relational Aesthetics*. Dijon: Les presses du réel, 2020.

Bratton, J S. "Dancing a Hornpipe in Fetters." *Folk Music Journal* 6, no. 1 (1990): 65–82.

Brown, Irving Henry. *Gypsy Fires in America: A Narrative of Life among the Romanies of the United States and Canada*. New edition. Port Washington, NY: Kennikat Press, 1972.

Brown, Russell Patrick. "'This Little Wooden World': Choreo-Navigating Maritime Dance." In *Celebrating Flamenco's Tangled Roots: The Body Questions*, edited by K. Meira Goldberg and Antoni Pizà, 1st edition. Newcastle upon Tyne: Cambridge Scholars Publishing, 2022.

Jean Butler's Irish Dance Master Class. Kultur Video, 2005.

Cancienne, Mary Beth, and Celeste N. Snowber. "Writing Rhythm: Movement as Method." *Qualitative Inquiry* 9, no. 2 (April 1, 2003): 237–53. https://doi.org/10.1177/1077800402250956.

Candlin, Fiona. "A Proper Anxiety: Practice-Based PhDs and Academic Unease." *Working Papers in Art and Design* 1, no. 1 (2000). http://eprints.bbk.ac.uk/archive/00000743.

Carson, Ciaran, trans. *The Táin*. Original edition. London: Penguin Classics, 2009.

Caruth, Cathy. *Unclaimed Experience: Trauma, Narrative and History*. 1st Edition. Baltimore, MD: Johns Hopkins University Press, 1996.

Cisneros, Rosemary, and Russell Patrick Brown. "Forbidden Movement : Historical and Contemporary Anti-Gypsyism in Dance and the Emergence of Romani Dance Studies." In *New Mobilities "on the Turn."* The Place, London, 2023.

Clandinin, D. Jean, and F. Michael Connelly. *Narrative Inquiry: Experience and Story in Qualitative Research*. 1st edition. San Francisco, CA: Jossey-Bass, 2004.

Cleveland Museum of Art. *Exhibition - Into the Light The Projected Image in American Art, 1964-1977*. Cleveland Museum of Art, 2002. http://archive.org/details/cmapr4449.

Cloitre, Marylene, Karestan C. Koenen, Lisa R. Cohen, and Hyemee Han. "Skills Training in Affective and Interpersonal Regulation Followed by Exposure: A Phase-Based Treatment for PTSD Related to Childhood Abuse." *Journal of Consulting and Clinical Psychology* 70, no. 5 (2002): 1067–74. https://doi.org/10.1037//0022-006X.70.5.1067.

Cloitre, Marylène. *Treating Survivors of Childhood Abuse Psychotherapy for the Interrupted Life*. New York, NY: Guilford Press, 2006.

Colvin, Geoff. *Talent Is Overrated: What Really Separates World-Class Performers from Everybody Else*. Updated edition. New York: Portfolio, 2010.

Cullinane, John P. *Irish Dancing Costumes: Their Origins and Evolution Illustrated with 100 Years of Photographs, 1892-1992*. Cork City: J.P. Cullinane, 1994.

Davis, Dominic-Madori. "A Viral Twitter Thread Is Asking What's Considered Trashy If You're Poor, but Classy If You're Rich — and Things like Donuts, Marrying Your Cousin, and Being Bilingual Are All Making the List." *Business Insider*, July 23, 2020. https://www.businessinsider.com/viral-twitter-thread-double-standards-between-rich-poor-trashy-classy-2020-7.

Davis, Lennard J., ed. *The Disability Studies Reader*. 4 edition. New York, NY: Routledge, 2013.

DeBhairduin, Oein. *Why the Moon Travels*. Dublin: Skein Press, 2020.

DeFrantz, Thomas F., and Anita Gonzalez, eds. *Black Performance Theory*. Durham, NC: Duke University Press, 2014.

DeFrantz, Thomas F. "Dancing in Blackface." In *FSU College of Fine Arts*. FSU School of Theatre, 2022. https://cfa.fsu.edu/symposium-on-global-blackface-global-minstrelsy-presented-by-fsu-school-of-theatre/.

DeFrantz, Thomas F. *Dancing Many Drums: Excavations In African American Dance*. Madison, WI: University of Wisconsin Press,

2002.

De Keersmaeker, Anne Teresa. *Fase, Four Movements to the Music of Steve Reich*. 1982. Performance by Anne Teresa De Keersmaeker, Kaaitheater, Brussels.

Dias, Brian G, and Kerry J Ressler. "Parental Olfactory Experience Influences Behavior and Neural Structure in Subsequent Generations." *Nature Neuroscience* 17, no. 1 (December 1, 2013): 89–96. https://doi.org/10.1038/nn.3594.

Dobai, Anna, and Nick Hopkins. "Hungarian Roma and Musical Talent: Minority Group Members' Experiences of an Apparently Positive Stereotype." *British Journal of Social Psychology*, September 4, 2020. https://doi.org/10.1111/bjso.12416.

Gallagher, Shaun. *How the Body Shapes the Mind*. 1st edition. Oxford: Clarendon Press, 2006.

Gallaí, Breandán de. "Imeall-Siúl: A Choreographic Exploration of Expressive Possibilities in Irish Step Dancing." University of Limerick, 2013. http://ulir.ul.ie.proxy.lib.ul.ie/handle/10344/3615.

Gareiss, Nicholas. "An Buachaillín Bán: Reflections on One Queer's Performance within Traditional Irish Music & Dance." In *Queer Dance*, edited by Clare Croft. Oxford; New York: Oxford University Press, 2017.

Gonzalez, Anita. Afro-Mexico : *Dancing between Myth and Reality*. Austin, TX: University of Texas Press, 2010.

Egenolf, Susan B. "Maria Edgeworth in Blackface: Castle Rackrent and the Irish Rebellion of 1798." *ELH* 72, no. 4 (Winter 2005): 845–69.

FRA. "Roma in 10 European Countries: Main Results: Roma Survey 2021." Luxembourg: Publications Office of the European Union, 2023.

Friel, Brian. *Translations: A Play*. London; Boston, MA: Farrar, Straus and Giroux, 1995.

Foley, Catherine E. *Step Dancing in Ireland: Culture and History*. New edition. Farnham; Burlington, VT: Ashgate, 2013.

German Central Foundation. "History of German Central." Accessed May 11, 2015. http://germancentralfoundation.com/history.html.

Gilroy, Paul. *The Black Atlantic: Modernity and Double-Consciousness*. Reissue edition. Cambridge, MA: Harvard University Press, 1993.

Giuvlipen. "ROMA FUTURISM," August 19, 2020. https://giuvlipen.com/en/roma-futurism/.

Gonzalez, Anita. *Afro-Mexico : Dancing between Myth and Reality*. Austin, TX: University of Texas Press, 2010.

Green, Penelope. "In the Village, Another Piece of the City's History Is Coming Down." *The New York Times*, December 22, 2022, sec. Real Estate. https://www.nytimes.com/2022/12/22/realestate/gay-street-nyc.html.

Goldberg, K. Meira. *Sonidos Negros: On the Blackness of Flamenco*. New York, NY: Oxford University Press, 2018.

Grosz, Elizabeth. "Feminism, Materialism, and Freedom." In *New Materialisms: Ontology, Agency, and Politics*, edited by Diana H. Coole and Samantha Frost. Durham, NC; London: Duke University Press, 2010.

Halberstam, Jack. *Wild Things: The Disorder of Desire*. Durham, NC: Duke University Press Books, 2020.

Hebdige, Dick. *Subculture, the Meaning of Style*. London: Methuen, 1979.

Iacci, Eromose. *The Crusaders: Hunt for the Sun Blade - Episode 1*. Independently published, 2022.

Jigs & Wigs - Viva Las Vegas!, 2014. https://www.youtube.com/watch?v=i__TmHgvj40&feature=youtube_gdata_player.

Johnson, Jasmine. "Black Laws of Dance." Edited by Anurima Banerji and Royona Mitra. *Decolonizing Dance Discourses*, Conversations Across The Field of Dance Studies, XL (2020): 25–27.

Joseph, May, and Sofia Varino. "Aquapelagic Assemblages: Performing Water Ecology with Harmattan Theater." *WSQ: Women's Studies*

Quarterly 45, no. 1–2 (2017): 151–66. https://doi.org/10.1353/wsq.2017.0021.

Jordan, Robert. *The Eye of the World: Book One of The Wheel of Time*. Media tie-in Edition. New York, NY: Tor Books, 2021.

Joyce, Sandra. " 'He Travelled East and He Travelled West…'– Travellers and 'Authenticity' in Irish Traditional Song." Paper presented at TradSong Symposium, University of Limerick, October 15, 2015.

Kennedy, John F. "Ich Bin Ein Berliner." June 26, 1963.

King-Dorset, Rodreguez. *Black Dance in London, 1730-1850 : Innovation, Tradition and Resistance*. Jefferson, NC: McFarland & Co., 2008.

Knorr Cetina, K. "Objectual Practice." In *The Practice Turn in Contemporary Theory*, edited by Theodore R Schatzki, Eike von Savigny, and K Knorr Cetina. London; New York, NY: Routledge, 2001.

L'Engle, Madeleine. *A Wrinkle in Time*. Reprint edition. New York, NY: Square Fish, 2007.

Lakoff, George, and Mark Johnson. *Metaphors We Live By*. 2nd edition. Chicago, IL: University of Chicago Press, 2003.

Lakoff, George, and Mark Johnson. *Philosophy in the Flesh: The Embodied Mind and Its Challenge to Western Thought*. Kindle. New York, NY: Basic Books, 2008.

Legendary. Reality-TV. Scout Productions, 2020.

Linebaugh, Peter, and Marcus Rediker. *The Many-Headed Hydra: Sailors, Slaves, Commoners, and the Hidden History of the Revolutionary Atlantic*. Boston, MA: Beacon Press, 2013.

Lyotard, Jean-François. *The Postmodern Condition: A Report on Knowledge*. 1st edition. Minneapolis, MN: University of Minnesota Press, 1984.

MacDonald, Shauna M. "Composing an Autoethnographic Cartography of Blue: Becoming a Pharologist in and of the Academy." *Cultural Studies – Critical Methodologies*, October 12, 2016, 1532708616673654. https://doi.

org/10.1177/1532708616673654.

Mark-FitzGerald, Emily. *Commemorating the Irish Famine: Memory and the Monument*. Liverpool: Liverpool University Press, 2013.

McLaughlin, Mary. "Lament of the Mermaid: An Mhaighdean Mhara - A Powerful Metaphor?" Paper presented at TradSong Symposium, University of Limerick, October 15, 2015.

Mercier, Mel. "Other Voices." Paper presented at *The Worlding of Irish Studies*, University of Notre Dame, April 1, 2016.

Melrose, Susan. "Confessions of an Uneasy Expert Spectator," 2007. http://www.sfmelrose.org.uk/.

Melrose, Susan. "Not yet, and Already No Longer: Loitering with Intent between the Expert Practitioner at Work, and the Archive." Somerset House, London, 2006. http://www.rescen.net/archive/PaK_may06/PaK06_transcripts4_1.html#.VkTI0soZ7Qx.

Mischke, Jan, Olivia White, Eckart Windhagen, Jonathan Woetzel, Michael Birshan, Sven Smit, Arvind Govindarajan, Szabolcs Kemeny, and Janet Bush. "The Future of Wealth and Growth Hangs in the Balance." McKinsey Global Institute, May 2023.

Millett, Kate. *Sexual Politics*. New York, NY: Columbia University Press, 2016.

Moloney, Mick, and John P. Harrington. "Harrigan, Hart, and Braham Irish America and the Birth of the American Musical." In *Irish Theater in America: Essays on Irish Theatrical Diaspora*. New York, NY: Syracuse University Press, 2009.

Moloney, Mick. "Irish-American Popular Music." In *Making the Irish American History and Heritage of the Irish in the United States*, edited by Marion R Casey and Joseph Lee. New York, NY: New York University Press, 2006.

Monaghan, Úna. "121 Stories: The Impact of Gender on Participation in Irish Traditional Music." *Ethnomusicology Ireland*, no. 7 (2021).

"The Lyric Feature: Common Ground," June 14, 2020. https://www.rte.ie/radio/radioplayer/html5/#/lyric/21430821.

"National Spiritualist Association of Churches." Accessed March 24, 2024. https://nsac.org/.

Ndiaye, Noémie. "Black Roma: Afro-Romani Connections in Early Modern Drama (and Beyond)." *Renaissance Quarterly* 75, no. 4 (2022): 1266–1302. https://doi.org/10.1017/rqx.2022.332.

Ndiaye, Noémie. *Scripts of Blackness: Early Modern Performance Culture and the Making of Race.* Edited by Geraldine Heng and Ayanna Thompson. Philadelphia, PA: University of Pennsylvania Press, 2022.

Nelson, Robin, ed. *Practice as Research in the Arts: Principles, Protocols, Pedagogies, Resistances.* Houndmills, Basingstoke, Hampshire: Palgrave Macmillan, 2013.

Newsome, Rashad. *Assembly*. The Armory Show, 2023, New York, NY.

Ní Shíocháin, Tríona. "Song as a Liminal Play Sphere: Aesthetics and Ideas/Taireachúlacht Agus Imeartas Na hAmhránaíochta: An Aeistéitic Agus an Machnamh." Paper presented at TradSong Symposium, University of Limerick, October 15, 2015.

Nimkulrat, Nithikul. "The Role of Documentation in Practice-Led Research." *Journal of Research Practice* 3, no. 1 (2007): 6.

Notes for Adjudicators. Prepared by Comhaltas Ceoltóirí Éireann as a Guide to Those Adjudicating Competitions for Irish Traditional Music and Singing at Fleadhanna Cheoil and Other CCE Functions. Dublin: Comhaltas Ceoltorí Éireann, 1987.

O'Brien, Cormac. "Gay Masculinities in Performance: Towards a Queer Dramaturgy." ITI 3, no. 1 (2014).

Obama, Michelle. *Becoming*. 1st edition. New York, NY: Crown, 2018.

Ohlmeyer, Jane. *Making Ireland English: The Irish Aristocracy in the Seventeenth Century.* New Haven, CT: Yale University Press, 2012.

Ono, Yoko. *Bag Piece*. 1964.

Ono, Yoko. *Cutting Piece*. 1964.

Ono, Yoko. *Sky TV*. 1966.

Ostadan, Bahar. "Holdout Tenant in $1,500 West Village Apartment Fears Demolition of Historic Townhouse." Gothamist, February 5, 2023, sec. News. https://gothamist.com/news/holdout-tenant-fears-1500-west-village-apartment-fears-demolition-of-historic-townhouse.

Ostendorf, Ann Marguerite. "Racializing American 'Egyptians': Shifting Legal Discourse, 1690s–1860s." *Critical Romani Studies* 2, no. 2 (December 2, 2020): 42–59. https://doi.org/10.29098/crs.v2i2.50.

Parry, Tyler D. *Jumping the Broom: The Surprising Multicultural Origins of a Black Wedding Ritual*. Kindle edition. Chapel Hill, NC: University of North Carolina Press, 2020.

Pickering, Andrew. "Practice and Posthumanism Social Theory and a History of Agency." In *The Practice Turn in Contemporary Theory*, edited by Theodore R Schatzki, K Knorr Cetina, and Eike von Savigny, 172–83. London; New York: Routledge, 2001. http://search.ebscohost.com/login.

Pose. Drama. Color Force, Brad Falchuk Teley-Vision, Ryan Murphy Television, 2018.

Preciado, Paul B. *Testo Junkie: Sex, Drugs, and Biopolitics in the Pharmacopornographic Era*. Translated by Bruce Benderson. New York, NY: The Feminist Press at CUNY, 2013.

Quaye, Stephen John. "Voice of the Researcher: Extending the Limits of What Counts as Research." *Journal of Research Practice* 3, no. 1 (2007): 13.

Ranciere, Jacques. *The Politics of Aesthetics: The Distribution of the Sensible*. Translated by Gabriel Rockhill. London ; New York, NY: Bloomsbury 3PL, 2006.

Regnault, Chantal. *Voguing and the House Ballroom Scene of New York, 1989-92*. Edited by Stuart Baker. 1st edition. London: Soul Jazz Records, 2011.

Reich, Steve. *Violin Phase*. Boosey & Hawkes, 1967.

Riach, Douglas C. "Blacks and Blackface on the Irish Stage, 1830–60." *Journal of American Studies* 7, no. 3 (December 1973): 231–41. https://doi.org/10.1017/S0021875800025299.

Rimmer, Joan. *The Irish Harp: Cláirseach na hÉireann.* 2nd edition. Dublin: The Mercer Press, 1977.

Ríos-Terheun, Victoria Eugenia. "The Question Is the Answer: Who Created Flamenco?" *FXB Center for Health & Human Rights | Harvard University* (blog), April 9, 2018. https://fxb.harvard.edu/2018/04/09/the-question-is-the-answer-who-created-flamenco/.

Robertson, Roland. *Globalization: Social Theory and Global Culture.* 1st edition. London: SAGE Publications Ltd, 1992.

Rodgers, Richard, and Oscar Hammerstein II. *Carousel.* Directed by Oliver Hurley, Killarney Music Society, 2008, Gleneagle INEC Arena, Killarney, Kerry, Ireland.

"Romani Realities in the United States: Breaking the Silence, Challenging the Stereotypes." Boston, MA: FXB Center for Health and Human Rights at Harvard University, November 2020.

RuPaul's Drag Race. Game-Show, Reality-TV. World of Wonder Productions, 2009.

Schechner, Richard, Peggy. "What Is Performance Studies Anyway?" In *The Ends of Performance*, edited by Peggy Phelan and Jill Lane. New York, NY: NYU Press, 1998.

Schrauwen, Isabelle, Béla I. Melegh, Imen Chakchouk, Anushree Acharya, Abdul Nasir, Alexis Poston, Diana M. Cornejo-Sanchez, et al. "Hearing Impairment Locus Heterogeneity and Identification of PLS1 as a New Autosomal Dominant Gene in Hungarian Roma." European Journal of Human Genetics 27, no. 6 (June 1, 2019): 869–78. https://doi.org/10.1038/s41431-019-0372-y.

Seaver, Michael. "'Concert' at Dublin Dance Festival: Warm, Funny, Respectful and Irreverent." *The Irish Times*, May 19, 2017. https://www.irishtimes.com/culture/stage/concert-at-dublin-dance-festival-warm-funny-respectful-and-irreverent-1.3089297.

Seibert, Brian. *What the Eye Hears: A History of Tap Dancing.* New York, NY: Farrar, Straus and Giroux, 2015.

Sexton, Ciara. 2020. "Well Done Orfhlaith Ni Bhriain" Facebook, November 25, 2020. https://www.facebook.com/watch/?v=374196856988804.

Shea Murphy, Jacqueline. *The People Have Never Stopped Dancing: Native American Modern Dance Histories*. Minneapolis, MN: University of Minnesota Press, 2007. https://muse.jhu.edu/pub/23/monograph/book/32234.

Shusterman, Richard. *Body Consciousness: A Philosophy of Mindfulness and Somaesthetics*. 1 edition. Cambridge ; New York, NY: Cambridge University Press, 2008.

Smith, Terry, and Kate Fowle. *Thinking Contemporary Curating*. New York, NY: Independent Curators International, 2012.

Sterne, Jonathan. The Audible Past: Cultural Origins of Sound Reproduction. Durham: Duke University Press Books, 2003.

Stewart, Bruce. "On the Necessity of De-Hydifying Irish Cultural Criticism." *New Hibernia Review/Iris Éireannach Nua*, 2000, 23–44.

Sullivan, Nikki. "Somatechnics." *TSQ: Transgender Studies Quarterly* 1, no. 1–2 (May 1, 2014): 187–90. https://doi.org/10.1215/23289252-2399983.

Swift, Jonathan. *A Tale of a Tub*. Edited by Henry Morley, 2003. https://www.gutenberg.org/ebooks/4737.

Taylor, Diana. *The Archive and the Repertoire*. Durham, NC: Duke University Press, 2003.

Taylor, Julie. *Paper Tangos*. Kindle Edition. Duke University Press, 2012.

Théleur, E. A. *Letters on Dancing, Reducing This Elegant and Healthful Exercise to Easy Scientific Principles*. London: Printed for the Author by Sherwood & Co. Image. https://www.loc.gov/item/05029181/.

Tomko, Linda J. "Bodies and Dances in Progressive-Era America." In *Dancing Class: Gender, Ethnicity, and Social Divides in American Dance, 1890-1920*, 1–35. Bloomington, IN: Indiana University Press, 1999.

Tosone, Carol. "Shared Trauma." In *Encyclopedia of Trauma*, edited by C. Figley. Thousand Oaks, CA: SAGE Publications, 2012.

Traoré, Rokia. *Sé Dan*. Nonesuch, 2016. MP3 download.

Varoufakis, Yanis. *Technofeudalism: What Killed Capitalism*. Brooklyn: Melville House, 2024.

Villeneuve, Denis. *Arrival*. Paramount Pictures, 2016.

VisualAIDS. "'The Luna Show Started Because I Got Tired of People Referencing Paris Is Burning….'" Visual AIDS, April 24, 2015. https://www.visualaids.org/blog/detail/luna-luis-ortiz-vava.

When the Rubber Meets the Dirt Road, 2015. https://www.youtube.com/watch?v=z1uCRFTo7ik.

Whitinui, Paul. "Indigenous Autoethnography: Exploring, Engaging, and Experiencing 'Self' as a Native Method of Inquiry." *Journal of Contemporary Ethnography* 43(4) (2013): 456–87.

Williams, W. H. A. 'Twas Only an Irishman's Dream: The Image of Ireland and the Irish in American Popular Song Lyrics, 1800-1920. Urbana: University of Illinois Press, 1996.

Woetzel, Jonathan, Jan Mischke, Anu Madgavkar, Eckart Windhagen, Sven Smit, Michael Birshan, Szabolcs Kemeny, and Rebecca J. Anderson. "The Rise and Rise of the Global Balance Sheet: How Productively Are We Using Our Wealth?" McKinsey Global Institute, November 2021. https://www.mckinsey.com/~/media/mckinsey/industries/financial%20services/our%20insights/the%20rise%20and%20rise%20of%20the%20global%20balance%20sheet%20how%20productively%20are%20we%20using%20our%20wealth/mgi-the-rise-and-rise-of-the-global-balance-sheet-full-report-vf.pdf.

Feeling Impact: